Praise for

The Christian in the Cult

Millions of religious believers will clearly recognize the spiritual journey narrated by Jim Valekis in this powerful story. A son of the Greek Orthodox Church finds himself in Herbert W. Armstrong's Worldwide Church of God, which eventually takes him into more traditional Christianity and out again. Where he ends up at the end of this fascinating pilgrimage will be a big surprise. But Valekis astutely narrates his journey and brings readers along with him to a spiritual destination that includes the whole world. In a religious and political landscape that has become a culture war of all against all, Valekis's final message of oneness and wholeness in Christ is a welcome antidote.
—**Andrew Manis,** Emeritus Professor of History *Middle Georgia State University, Macon, Georgia*

***

In your hands is a book that speaks powerfully to both the complexities of living and growing in the Church, and to the way God moves in our individual lives as believers. Through the story of author Jim Valekis, we see a riveting faith testimony passed from one generation of family to another -- across cultures, continents, and denominations. We experience through Jim's journey how our Christian faith can ground us and cover us spiritually, despite a fallen world, broken relationships, and vocational volatility. Jim reminds us that while our conditions and surroundings rise and fall, our steadfast relationship with Christ is All. I commend this book to you.
—**Chuck Proudfit,** President *At Work On Purpose*

***

Jim Valekis has written a journey narrative that bends the reader continually toward wholeness in Christ. His writing is deeply personal, clearly theological, and thoroughly biblical, mining the depth of each discipline to unearth the force of God's transforming love. There is in these pages a complex personal story, interwoven with historical and scriptural insights that can guide the reader through the fog of theological compromise to the clarity that comes when Christ alone is the Lord of life. It has been said that life is a journey of formation, with the looming question, "Into what am I being formed?" Jim Valekis shines an uncompromising light on the person of Jesus Christ and bids us to surrender to the formative power of his Presence, alive in the human heart.

—**Terry Wardle,** Founder of Healing Care Ministries, Author of *From Broken to Beloved,* and *Some Kind of Crazy*

***

Jim Valekis is a great (and funny!) storyteller whose message for all of us is embedded in his epic journey! Through the lens of his late-coming theological discovery, Valekis guides us on his profound and sometimes painful path through three distinct expressions of faith-- his Greek Orthodox roots, Herbert Armstrong's Worldwide Church of God, and modern-day Evangelicalism-- and demonstrates the abiding presence of Jesus Christ through it all. This book will encourage any reader who desires to explore how every person's identity as a beloved child of God is deeper than any doctrine, Christian or otherwise.

—**Jeff McSwain**

Founder of Reality Ministries, Author of *Movements of Grace: The Dynamic Christo-Realism of Barth, Bonhoeffer and the Torrances, 'Simul' Sanctification: Barth's Hidden Vision for Human Transformation,* and of a soon-to-be-released two-volume work of Systematic Theology for Systemic Change *Volume 1: Hidden in Contradiction: Humanity in Christ Before, During, and After the Fall*
Volume 2: The Goodness of Judgement: The Ministry of Christ's Cross for a Hurting World (upcoming in 2024)

THE
CHRISTIAN
IN THE
CULT

AND HOW I DISCOVERED

HUMANITY IN CHRIST

JIM VALEKIS

Published by KHARIS PUBLISHING, an imprint of KHARIS MEDIA LLC.

Copyright © 2024 Jim Valekis

ISBN-13: 978-1-63746-246-1

ISBN-10: 1-63746-246-8

Library of Congress Control Number: 2024931139

Scripture quotations taken from the New International Version, Copyright 1973, 1978, 1984, 2011 by Biblica, Inc. appear as NIV.

Scripture quotations taken from the King James Version cited on Biblegateway.com, Public Domain, appear as KJV.

Scripture quotations taken from the New King James Version®, Copyright 1982 by Thomas Nelson, appear as NKJV.

Scripture quotations taken from the New Revised Standard Version Bible: Anglicised Edition, Copyright 1989, 1995 the Division of Christian Education of the National Council of the Churches of Christ in the United States of America, appear as NRSVA.

All KHARIS PUBLISHING products are available at special quantity discounts for bulk purchase for sales promotions, premiums, fund-raising, and educational needs. For details, contact:

Kharis Media LLC
Tel: 1-630-909-3405
support@kharispublishing.com
www.kharispublishing.com

CONTENTS

PART 1:
MY FIRST CULT

Why was my doctrinally "orthodox" church not able to go the distance and take me compellingly into a life with God through Scriptural engagement? Why did I have to go to a cult to experientially find Christ?

PART 2:
THE LOST WORLD OF THE WORLDWIDE CHURCH OF GOD

What was it like in this "cult" in its pre-change heyday? This shares the story of a Lost World of a uniquely culturally and spiritually connected people. It is a story of a world of belonging that many who lived through feel has never been equaled in mainstream, "non-cult" Christianity. There was an epic, heady sense of uniqueness experienced in the cult. And it wasn't all bad.

PART 3:
THE RECONSTRUCTION YEARS

Pastoring in the Worldwide Church of God through the years of doctrinal reformation is a fascinating study that proves one thing. Cultural transformation, even when necessary, is going to be very hard—and takes a long, long time.

PART 4:
OUT OF THE FIRE INTO THE FRYING PAN

What happens when a whole culture based on a "wrong" interpretation of the Scripture begins to realize the truth? What was it like stepping into newfound freedoms in Christ? What joys were discovered? What new griefs—and cultic issues—were discovered in American Evangelicalism?

PART 5:
CULTS IN COLLISION

Does doctrinal truth really transform—or does it simply reform? And what happens to early adopters in a climate of sluggish cultural reform?

PART 6:
THE MOST INSIDIOUS CULT

What was the most potentially limiting cult in this journey from cult to cult to cult? Why is this one potentially the most insidious? How might it affect all of us in "American" Christianity more than we realize?

PART 7:
WHAT DOES IT MEAN TO BE A CHRISTIAN IN CHRIST?

A new old way (neo-orthodox) of looking at what makes us Christians in the first place and how many more people may be included than we realize.

PART 8:
APPENDIX

PREFACE

CULTIC CHRISTIANITY

I was a Christian in a cult. For forty years I was in the Worldwide Church of God, founded by Herbert W. Armstrong, which many regarded at best to be a fringe, non-orthodox "sect" and at worst, a dangerous cult. In 1994, the Worldwide Church of God (WCG) reformed doctrinally in a headline-making way and began to reject its former heretical beliefs. In 1997 WCG was accepted into the National Association of Evangelicals and in 2009 changed its name to Grace Communion International (GCI). For 28 years I was a WCG pastor and then a GCI pastor, doing what I thought was best to lead others in the way of Christ.

How did a kid raised in the Greek Orthodox Church end up in the Worldwide Church of God at age fifteen? And now, looking back down the timeline of my spiritual pilgrimage, how do I explain these two major themes: 1) that even though I was in a cult for decades with WCG, my season in the Greek Orthodox Church *before* WCG, and my season in Evangelicalism *after* WCG, also had at least some of the markings of a cult and 2) how do I explain the undeniable presence of Christ in the midst of all of these religious expressions?

The word "cult" can be scary. When I told my sister that I was writing a memoir entitled "The Christian in the Cult," she suggested I might use a less polarizing and more toned-down word. It's a word that carries a lot of scary baggage, for sure.

An article entitled "17 of the Most Terrifying Cults in History" by Hristina Byrnes[1] catalogs some of the "big names" in groups known as cults in our era. The author's description is purely pejorative: "Official dictionaries define 'cult' as a religion regarded as unorthodox or spurious, such as satanic cults. Another definition is a misplaced or excessive admiration for a particular person or thing. In many of the more extreme cults, a charismatic leader charms, some say brainwashes, members to follow an unconventional religion and set of rules. Occasionally you'll hear or read of someone referencing a 'satanic' cult or a 'voodoo' cult. Many religions have been called a 'dangerous' cult, deservedly so."

I'm not sure which "official dictionaries" Byrnes is referring to, but we must quickly add that "cult" is not automatically a bad word. The Merriam-Webster Dictionary has two definitions of cult: 1) "a group of people showing intense devotion to a cause, person, or work (as a film)" and 2) "a body of beliefs and practices regarding the supernatural and the worship of one or more deities."[2] These more mundane definitions of cult are reflected in Old Testament studies, for instance, where it is not at all uncommon to talk about the "cultic practices" of Israel. These practices are succinctly stated in Psalm 51.

Then you will delight in the sacrifices of the righteous, in burnt offerings offered whole; then bulls will be offered on your altar. (Psalm 51:19, NIV)[*]

Those are cultic practices. Of course, those worshipping Baal and other gods also had their own cultic practices.

I would put my experience in the Worldwide Church of God somewhere between the pejorative and mundane definitions of cult above. Herbert Armstrong was no Jim Jones or David Koresh, but it's also true (as put forth in both the Byrnes and Merriam-Webster definitions) that WCG exalted the leadership of a single personality whose word was in many ways "gospel," and that this charismatic person elicited a reverential following and expected an unquestioned commitment to the cause.

Aside from an allegiance to Armstrong that was borderline, if not in some cases flat-out idolatrous, our cult shared the basic qualities of other modern and ancient cultic expressions. Namely, along with initiation markers for entry, a cult typically adheres to a strict set of beliefs or doctrinal principles that are meant to distinguish it from other expressions. There is a deep conviction that "our way of doing things" is right, and others' ways are wrong. This breeds an insular "group-think," and a hubris that exalts one's group as the shining "city upon a hill" that will light the way for all those who wander in darkness. It's our light, and their darkness. *That's why to be in a cult—or to be*

---

*This Scripture and the majority of the Scriptural citations in this work are from the New International Version (NIV) of the Bible, properly cited in the Works Cited section found at the end of this work. Scriptures quoted from other translations are noted, and are properly cited in the Works Cited section as well.

even in a church or sect that manifests and promotes (actively or passively) its cultic practices or "culture" more than Christ— is to put major emphasis on an "us vs them" perspective.

I see these symptoms strongly manifested in our time in WCG under Armstrong's teaching, and I also see some of these symptoms in my Greek Orthodox and Evangelical experience before and after Armstrong. Without realizing it, many of us outside of an acknowledged "cult" may be guilty of either actively or passively imposing cultural or "cultic" conditions upon people that prevent their coming to faith in Christ. We may be more focused on bringing people to our "church" or our "culture" than we are on bringing them to an awareness of the Christ *in us all*—including the Christ already with them and in them, whether they know it or not.

We find comfort in our sub-group's "doctrine." In fact, I can hear some saying, "Well, in order to have a group or a sub-culture or a denomination of Christian faith there is always going to be a built-in 'us vs them.'" But is that really the case? Is there a way that the Christian faith can articulate its sacraments and conversion markers with a less judgmental posture? Can we embrace a Christ-centered worldview that actually disallows an "us vs them?"

Notice carefully what Paul says about his own conversion. While he was going to destroy Christians in the name of Judaism, his "cult" (Galatians 1:11-15), God revealed something astounding to Him. Paul says God was pleased to reveal His Son—"in me!" (verse 16). Not *to* me but *in* me! Did that mean the Son was already *in* him—even though he didn't even realize it and had never given him permission to be there?

Even in my WCG days, when I was absorbed in the most radical "us against the world" mentality, I was being pulled towards a mindset of more. I gradually discovered the life-giving difference between seeing humans in cultic categories and seeing humanity in Christ and Christ in humanity. This allows me to look back and to see the good, right, and true expressions of Christ in all the cults I've participated in.

Ironically, in my journey from cult to cult to cult I also began to realize that cultic refers less to a group of people and more to a way of thinking. Because all three of my cult group experiences had a "God's one true church" mentality, the us vs them was easier to see. In the end, I have to admit that this us vs them mindset is one that continually lurks in my own sinful flesh. Only in the Spirit can I rise above carnal cult-think.

To add irony to irony, it's increased assurance of humanity in Christ (a humanity that includes me!) that gives me an increased awareness of my sin. In the light of God's grace, I can better stand against the sin which continually entangles. Against the darkness I am seeking to walk in the light, to follow Paul as he learned from Christ, and "to no longer look at anyone from a worldly point of view" (2 Corinthians 5:16).

In the pages that follow I reflect on what I have learned. I offer it that it might potentially benefit the church at large as it seeks to remain hopeful and prophetic in a turbulent, conflicted world. This book is about my journey to discovery, and my journeys within my journey.

Chapter 1

HOW GREEK

WAS MY VALLEY

A short narrative of my family of origin's history might shed light on why I was poised for future cultic affiliations that would be a part of my life journey for so long.

I was born in Alabama with a bouzouki on my knee. In case you're unfamiliar with the song "O Susanna," that means I was born to a Greek-American family in Birmingham, Alabama. Birmingham had a thriving Greek community that resulted in the building of a magnificent Greek Orthodox cathedral in its midst. The first Greek immigrant moved to the city in 1865 and word began to spread with other Greeks looking for a home in America.

My father's family was one of them. Like many Greek immigrants of that generation, they were entrenched deeply in a culture within a culture. They were Greeks first, Americans second. And undeniably, they belonged to God's "one true church." It would be the first of several "one true church" expressions I would belong to before all was said and done.

Dad's Side of the Family

My father's family made its way to Birmingham in the early 1900s. I still remember finding a listing of their home on 17th Street South in the 1917 edition of the Birmingham City Directory at the Birmingham Public Library. My grandfather was listed as "Charles Valekis" (an Americanized version of Hathouli Vavleki, his real name) and a grocer.

His wife, my grandmother, was listed as "Jewel." Her name wasn't Jewel though. It was Julia in "American" (really, Ioulia pronounced ee-oo-lee'-ah in Greek). But I guess in a land of southern dialects and Greek immigrants doing their best to be understood, Jewel was what some door-to-door city canvasser heard and decided was good enough to record.

All Greeks have their American names, and then their real ones—their Greek names. Who they really are is who they are in Greek. From the get-go, we were taught to live in a world within a world. We were *in* America but not *of* America. Our real world was the Greek one. The Greeks had God's "one true church." No matter how far you had to drive, you would drive to get to God's one true church, with God's one true people. I imagine we all are prone to cultural superiority issues to some degree. I've learned that it takes a while for us to learn how to discern our uniqueness in the context of the shared uniqueness of others, and not in contrast or superiority to others.

My grandfather the grocer had come to America working on a boat shoveling coal into the boilers that fueled the big ships. He was from the northern part of Greece near the towns called Larissa and Veria, the latter of which I believe is the biblical Berea of Acts 17. These people were famous for their "more noble" attitude when it came to the study of Scripture, as Acts 17:11 relates. They were also famous for a meal called *spanaki avgolemono*, a lesser-known version of the better-known Greek *avgolemono* (egg and lemon) soup made with rice, egg, and chicken broth. The *spanaki* (spinach) version, believe it or not, has the same frothy egg and lemon mixture but replaces the rice with spinach and adds tomato sauce. It makes spinach palatable. Even as kids, we liked it.

My grandfather was an intense man, as one aunt described him: forceful, earthy, and gruff. He died in the Influenza Epidemic of 1926 which claimed 500,000 lives. He did not die because the flu killed him. He died because he impetuously seized a bottle of medicine on his nightstand and drank it all in one impulsive gulp to hasten his recovery. This did not hasten his recovery. It hastened his death. The medicine did something to his bile duct, and he died shortly thereafter. My father, just five years old at the time, found him dead in his bed.

My grandmother "Jewel" (Julia) had already been widowed once before in Greece. Soon after her first husband's death, she made her journey to America with a five-year-old daughter, a three-year-old son, and a baby on the way---to whom she gave birth on the boat before the journey was completed. She eventually married my grandfather and had four more children (my dad was the third one). When grandfather died, she was left to raise my five-year-old father and his baby sister alone. She died unexpectedly of a stroke before she could bring them to maturity. Again, my dad, this time in his mid-teens, was the one who found her dead in her bed.

Having been the one who found both parents in this way impacted Dad, I think, pushing his mind toward the larger questions of life. And as the youngest son, Dad had more years to benefit from my grandmother's kindly influence. Growing into adulthood he developed a deep God-consciousness. Except for the time he served in the Navy during World War Two, Dad stayed close to home, establishing a deep network of friends. His devotion to God and the Greek Church would become legendary in our Birmingham community. It was standing room only at his funeral in 2009. "That man changed my life," more than one former altar boy said. Dad had a noble heart, like his Berean forebears before him. He didn't just study his Bible. He lived it.

We grew up with a deep reverence for the Bible. Mama was almost superstitious about it, in a Greek village girl way. If we accidentally dropped it on the floor, we had to kiss it in an act of atonement. Dad was very pious about the Holy Scriptures. He had a special Bible given to him by one of the founding Greek Orthodox priests in the city. It was particularly holy, and always kept in our small, inexpensive, antiqued green bookcase. I would get to hold it and read it sometimes. I remember the "mystery" of trying to track the tiny little Scriptural reference "footnotes" in the column in between the two-columned text of this sacred "old-style" Bible. It was special to me, too.

In my Greek Orthodox experience, we revered Holy Scripture. We stood in solemn attention when the priest majestically carried the silver-gilt Bible out of the altar at the liturgy flanked by altar boys and candles. The Bible wasn't just mystically or even superstitiously holy either. It was holy in "the whole"—in its entirety. Everything in it was true and hence to be observed from cover to cover. Like many Christians, we didn't know the difference between the Old Covenant and the New. Whatever the Bible said to do, in either half, you were to do. We did not know how to rightly divide the word of truth. We never heard in-depth teachings that enabled us to discern which observances held more weight than others.

Perhaps that's why, when I left the Greek Orthodox fold, I was so vulnerable to Herbert Armstrong's teachings about keeping the seventh-day Sabbath. After all, it is the only weekly worship day commanded in the Scripture.

Mama's Side of the Family

Mama was smart, tough, and compassionate. And coming from a region near Sparta, she was a true Spartan mother. She was fiercely loyal, and what she loved, she loved intensely and defensively. And she could rise above tragedy and loss and make life work for her. She had lovely oval green eyes, what my cousin calls "Spartan eyes." They were set in high cheekbones and a classically oval face. But her eyes conveyed more than just beauty. They conveyed intelligence and the same Spartan tenacity her village ancestors had exhibited for generations (like when they fled to the mountains to survive the Ottoman invasion in the 15th century). It would take the forces of World War Two and post-war Communism in Greece to uproot Mama from her homeland.

Mama was an original, and that's no exaggeration. Her name was Maria Pagona Stratakis, and she went by the name Pagona in the Greek community. By the way, you're not pronouncing Pagona correctly, no matter how you're pronouncing it in your mind as you read this name. The Greek "g" is an unusual, soft sound coupled with an "h" ("gh"). I have heard no equivalent in English for it, and Americans find it very difficult to master. This soft "g" sound is so subtle that when non-Greek ears hear it, the best they can do to emulate it is to make a "w" sound. Couple that with the fact that the "o" in the middle is a Greek "o." This vowel has neither a long nor a short sound. It is an "o" sound deep in the base of your throat, the sound you make when you're attempting to imitate an Eastern meditation chant. It's the sound you hear in the "oh oh oh's" of Billy Joel's "For the Longest Time." It's basically butchered by non-Greek-speaking Americans, especially in the South. They rushed through it without being aware of the musical high and low notes that are so much a part of the spoken Greek language.

Hence Mama was never known as Pagona to our Southern neighbors. She was not even known as Maria, which was her real first name. She was known simply as Marie. But she was Pagona in the rarefied atmosphere of the Greek community.

Again, we lived in a world within a world. In Mama's mind, the Greek language, and the Greeks in general, were superior to anything and everything else around them. This quick-minded, quick-witted, savvy Greek village girl still identified with her ancient culture's penchant for assuming (benevolently) that all non-Greeks were, well, barbarians. I can still remember her telling me how "babies in Greece are 'much more fatter' [sic] than babies in America."

14

That meant they were fed better food, and thus were infinitely healthier than the children of these badly accented country people who didn't know how to feed their children. I remember her telling me I was so lucky to have a Greek mother, because if Miss Iris (the red-haired lady two houses down from us) was my mother, we'd be eating pinto beans three times a day.

She truly believed in our Greek cultural superiority. And we truly believed her. We were not only Orthodox—we were Greek. And this passionate ambassador sold us on both.

A Sheltered World in an Epic Context

Mama's father, one of five siblings, was born in 1886 in the Peloponnesus region of Greece. I know very little about his upbringing except for two stories Mama shared with me. One story was of how his younger sister Olga lost her life attempting to cross rapids in a churning river near their village. Another story was how his father (my great-grandfather) died when my grandfather was only twelve. My grandfather ("Papou" in Greek) was awakened in the dark by his mother the morning after the funeral. She put a lantern into his hand. She told him not to come home until he found work. And he didn't. He looked for work so resourcefully that he ended up in the United States of America in 1906, where he eventually ran some type of *magazi* (store). I'm guessing it was a combination diner, grocery store, and coffee shop.

What an amazing time that must have been. The city was welcoming resourceful immigrants from all quarters, and America was indeed the land of opportunity. For the Greeks, it was also the land of new cultural experiences and new cultural horizons. There is a picture of Papou holding up toy guns in some kind of vaudeville play and wearing a cowboy hat to boot. With his Cupid's bow Greek lips, heavy-lidded eyes, and a roundish face, he wasn't a very convincing cowboy. But I'm impressed that he tried.

He brought his sister Cornelia over to live with him in America as well. Mama told the story that one time he was in trouble with one of his creditors, and he ran rapidly into the apartment he shared with her to hide from them. He ran by her and said hurriedly, in Greek, "Don't tell them anything. Say I'm not here. I'm going to be in the closet." "Thea," (Aunt) Cornelia, didn't hear the "Don't tell them anything" part, and, unbeknownst to him, she'd been practicing her English. So, when the creditors knocked on the door, she proudly announced, "He's-a not-a here. He's-a in the closet." I can only imagine what happened next.

It came time for Papou to be married, so apparently "they" (whoever "they" were) picked out a bride for him. But the day he met the woman arranged for him he also saw Vasiliki Sabbatako, who eventually would become my grandmother. "I don't want this one," he said about the other lady after seeing my grandmother who was several years his junior. Pointing to my grandmother, he said, "I want that one." And in this strongly patriarchal society, he got that one. He married her, and they prospered living in their apartment at 518 Flatbush in Brooklyn.

I don't know the cause—maybe more incidents like the "in the closet" scene, financial difficulties, or health issues—but the official story is that because of his "health," his doctor recommended that they move back to Greece. So, in the early 1930s, just in time to miss the worst of the Great Depression, Papou and "Yiayia" (grandmother in Greek) made the return voyage to Greece with six or seven-year-old Mama and her three older brothers in tow. For several years they lived in the enviable position of the family of a father who'd made it in America and now came back home to live prosperously in his hometown village. He built what Mama described as a beautiful house with balconies and exquisite furniture. They ran a village store from a room on the ground level. It had the only indoor bathroom in the village, Mama proudly recounted. He brought electricity to the village too, erecting something called "The Lux" which, when I saw it on my trip to Greece in the early 2000s, looked like a tiny Eiffel Tower strung with electric wires. It helped bring the village a bit of modern technology and powered the one television my grandmother, kerchiefed Greek old lady style, would go to years later in a local café to watch her favorite American show, "The Wild Wild West."

Papou and Yiayia had one more daughter shortly after their move to Greece. They were at the top of their game in the little village world they lived in—a beautiful home, financially prosperous, cheerful children. It was a life romanticized and idealized by mother—and lost dramatically and tragically because of the maniacal machinations of Adolph Hitler and Benito Mussolini.

World War Two – Lives Disrupted, Lives Displaced

Mussolini tried but failed to conquer Greece. Then Hitler sent the Nazi troops in April of 1941. He brutally conquered the nation and changed their lives forever. I'll let Mama tell the story of what happened when the Nazi blitzkrieg stormed through her village. She was skilled at storytelling, so imagine hearing a woman with a broken heart and yet a survivor's voice of acceptance and resoluteness telling you this story:

"I had to stop school in the 8th grade because of the war. We stayed home. We had to learn to make things for ourselves. That's when I learned how to knit socks. The night the Germans came, Baba [*Greek for Daddy*] had to take me and my sister to the mountains for safety. Mama couldn't go with us. She had just given birth to my youngest sister. She had to go into the woods and gnaw roots to survive and have enough strength to make milk for the baby. We didn't see her or know whether she was alive for a week.

"We fled and walked in snow that came up to our knees. We lived in the sewers for one week with only one loaf of bread to share among us. One time I tried to rest and sit down. But someone yelled, "Watch out!" I was about to sit on a dead body.

"When we came back, we saw more dead bodies. There were bodies of people hanging on the trees lining the roads to our village. People had even been hung from The Lux in front of our house. We couldn't go into our home. It was the best house in the village. The Germans used it for their headquarters. They destroyed everything— our furniture, our photographs, our pictures, our memories. They left nothing.

"We had to live in the 'summer house.' (*This was a small shack of a shelter where they sometimes lived when harvesting olives*). A British soldier came to us one time and was looking for help. My mother helped him. She would not turn him away. They could have killed her for doing this if they found out. But she did it anyway.

"The Germans took the boys in the village, and we thought they were going to kill them. My brother Aleco, (Alex) was among them. Somehow, he managed to live. And he let my mother know he was alive by whistling a tune he knew she'd recognize as the soldiers marched them near the village."

When the tide of the war turned, the family was able to reoccupy their own home, ravaged though it was. The little store on the first level found a new use. It became a British prison for the defeated and captured Nazi soldiers.

By this time Mama was a beautiful young woman near twenty. She remembers ignoring them in their jail in spite of their incessant beckoning, "Fraulein, Fraulein come here."

Eventually, new internal battles rocked the destabilized and barely surviving nation. Her father was what she called a Democrat, meaning he was not a communist. But the villagers who were militant communists were insistent. They were recruiting all Greek women to become *andartinas*, women guerilla fighters for the Communist Party. They rounded up my grandmother and mother to "recruit" them. Recruitment included beating my mother on the back with their rifle butts.

This all had taken a toll on Mama, one I think that troubled her in various ways all her life. She started to smoke. It was "to calm" her fears, she would explain in later years.* Her father knew it was time to act. After all, she was born in America, and she was an American citizen. He had stores in America he could sell to help rebuild their home in the village. It was time to go to America and sell the stores and to take Mama to live safely with his sister Cornelia, who by now lived in some place called Alabama.

The Journey to America

Having made arrangements for his family's safety in Greece while he was gone, Papou booked passage on the Queen Mary for him and Mama. The journey included a stop in Rome. Papou bought Mama a beautiful amethyst and cameo necklace which is one of my proudest possessions today. Mama would speak dismissively when I told her how beautiful and special I thought it was. "Eine pseftikou" she would say with a shrug of her shoulders. "It's fake." It still looks like a beautiful vintage piece to me, and it is a treasure from her epic journey to America. And as you read how I convey these stories, you can see the "epic" way I learned how to perceive my life.

Onboard the ship, Mama caught the eye of a wealthy Greek businessman who asked my grandfather for her hand in marriage. She was just that pretty. She

---

* This habit in all likelihood claimed her life. She "calmed" her nervousness by smoking for years, until she nearly died of emphysema in her latter years. But it was too late. Even though she lived several smoke-free years later, an aggressive lung cancer spot was missed at a physical because of the scars from the emphysema, and four months later she was diagnosed to be consumed with Stage 4 cancer that claimed her life two days after its diagnosis. I guess one way or another, she too was part of World War Two's death toll.

said no, and Papou said no, too. But perhaps it was an encouraging sign of good things to come.

She was filled with wide-eyed wonder at New York City. And New York City was filled with wide-eyed post-war wonder at her. Department store people suggested that she model. But she was only at her first stop in America. Birmingham, Alabama was the final destination. She cried when the train pulled into post-war Birmingham. It seemed like nothing compared to New York City. It began to sink in: she was going to be stuck there, perhaps forever.

Once you came to America in those days and under those conditions, more than likely you never returned to Greece. She left the life of innocence, wonder, status, and "place" she held in the village. She didn't speak a word of English and was too proud to sound "dumb" when she talked until she perfected it. She no longer had the place of belonging and stature that she once had. She was no longer a beautiful big fish in a very small pond. She was just one of the millions that were displaced by a horrible war. Papou returned to Greece as soon as he safely deposited her in New York City and conducted the business he had come to conduct. Even though she was living with "Thea" (Aunt) Cornelia, she desperately missed her mother and father. Mama lived in this American world but could never be *of* this American world. She was part of a Greek heaven from which she was tragically separated.

After she met my father, he would attempt to create a safe world for this broken beauty to live in, and for us to live in it with her. He simultaneously created in us a hunger and respect for orthodoxy and a hunger and respect for high achievement. Mom, on the other hand, instilled in us a longing for a home and heritage from which she was violently uprooted, one that still fueled the visionary fire of her life. In our tightly guarded world, we shared that epic vision with her. It created the fascinating atmosphere in which we grew up.

We were in the world, and not of it. It's no wonder a search for a place of belonging would be a part of my development from a very early age. I was stewed in a pot of over-protection, overachievement, cultural self-awareness, and cultural exclusion. This funnily dressed immigrant kid in a blue-collar, white, Anglo-Saxon Protestant post-World War Two world of a still segregated very southern town would find plenty of reasons to long for more in an epic, worldwide kind of way.

This is where the Birmingham Greek Community and the tiny Alabama neighborhood called Green Acres come in.

Chapter 2

BROKEN ENGLISH: LIVING AS STRANGERS IN A

STRANGE LAND

In the neighborhood I now live in just north of Dayton, Ohio, an influx of Muslim Russian-Turkish immigrants has moved in, much to the chagrin of some of the long-time inhabitants of this rural county. The immigrants bring with them their rich and tragic history. After facing centuries of persecution and cruel resettlements in Stalin's Russia, it is ironic that they now find themselves nestled in the midst of a homogenous Midwest farm culture that is not traditionally a welcoming place for "outsiders."

I go out of my way to be kind to these neighbors, especially the children. I want them to feel welcomed and accepted. I don't want them to grow up feeling too different, feeling too left out, especially since they are looked upon warily by some of my more conservative neighbors. I don't want them to be tilted toward some sort of cultic social self-defensiveness or the unintended sense of alienation that arises when different cultures live side by side. And frankly, I want to do what Christ wants us to do, which is to be kind to strangers in his name.

Sometimes, when my wife Becky and I take walks, we'll see some of their little boys out playing. They have big eyes, close-cropped hair, and frankly look like they come from a decidedly different gene pool than the other kids in the neighborhood. These boys were especially interested in (and afraid of) our now dearly-departed dog, a seventeen-pound chihuahua-terrier-chow mix. I smile thinking of the game they played with us, edging closer and closer to the dog, then scattering with abandon in every direction, calling out "Allah! Allah!"

These little guys remind me of me when I was a little boy growing up in the edge-of-town Birmingham neighborhood called, of all things, Green Acres. It was a modest blue-collar steel-working community. I was big-eyed and had close-cropped hair. Even my head was shaped differently (I guess it still is. A friend of mine recently visited the Pompeii exhibit that had come to town and observed, "They have heads like Pastor Jim"). To make me even more different as a youngster, my loving immigrant mother dressed me like the little boys would have been dressed in her village. I was not going to be a regular boy in Green Acres Elementary School.

For me (hearkening back to the theme song of a popular 1960s sitcom), Green Acres was—and wasn't—the place to be, because my experience there was part of the reason I became first a Christian and then one in a cult.

How We Got There

When Dad returned home from serving in the Navy in World War II, he and many of his peers found wives in the Greek community and began building their lives. Dad had grown up with dozens of second-generation Greek girls in Birmingham, but the arrival of my mom into the community put an end to fishing in that pond.

They were married in 1947 in a small little Greek church in North Birmingham that was the ancestor of the larger cathedral built a few years later. I'm not sure who gave her away. But Daddy took her and loved her as fiercely as any man could love a woman for the rest of his life.

Dad had chosen not to be a food truck driver or a hot dog stand owner like many of his prosperous peers in the Greek community in Birmingham. Those Greeks were packing it in and eventually lived in the most expensive neighborhoods in town. Dad, always the different one, was taking another approach. Dad chose to go to college (I imagine thanks to the GI Bill) to be an engineer and a frugal one who lived very modestly at that. He didn't move his growing little family into the better neighborhoods his peers were all working their way into. He first moved his family into government housing near downtown and the church while he got his degree. It was called Central City. Nobody used the real name "Metropolitan Gardens," because it was anything but. It was considered an area to be avoided, especially at night.

This context factored into my own birth. When Mama went into labor, Dad couldn't get anyone to come and stay with my two-year-old older brother so he could go to the hospital with my still non-English-speaking mom. So, he put Mama into a taxi on a very rainy Wednesday night at 9 pm and sent her to the hospital with a very kind taxi driver who she reported kept telling her, "Don't worry little lady! Don't worry little lady! I'm going to take care of you." Apparently, he did, and I was born and reunited with my father and brother and eventually joined by a little sister and later a little brother as well.

When Dad did get his degree, that's when we moved to Green Acres. It was on the edge of town near no other Greeks. But the house's backyard had a gate that opened to the elementary school, and since Mama had not (and would not) learn to drive, we had to walk to school where Mama could watch us leave from the kitchen window and watch for us to return home. She was very protective like a very Greek Spartan mother hen. Every day we were sent to school, commissioned by Dad to be the smartest kids in the class and representatives of our hard-working and superior ethnic heritage. We were Greeks first, Americans second. We always made A's. Anything else was unacceptable. And for some reason, it was not in our thought process to even consider playing (more than casually) with American children. At least it wasn't in mine.

This social "us" and "them" consciousness was most likely intensified by my mother's premature transfer to a culture in which she was still finding her bearings. For whatever reason, outside of school, we didn't play with the other kids. At least I didn't, not in our early years. We stayed at home, ate Greek food, and watched television but only after we did our homework practically the minute we got home from school.

I remember watching kids through our fence in neighboring yards playing with each other, longing to join them, but not knowing how. I remember participating in school with a bit of self-imposed arm's length detachment, in part, I'm sure, from the lack of social integration skills instilled in us by our insular environment. My mom was still a bit afraid of this American world and its society, so I was also to a certain degree.

That was our world—a culture within a culture—all nestled in the overarching reality of a very real God who was part of life.

The Day I Came to Jesus---or rather, Jesus Came to Me

A significant, life-altering event occurred during this period. It happened sometime between the second and fourth grades. My classmates apparently had had enough of this big-eyed Greek immigrant boy in their white Anglo-Saxon Protestant midst. The kids on the playground gathered around me and intentionally ganged up on me, the funny-looking immigrant boy with big eyes and red lips (redder that day because I'd been chewing on my red colored pencil) who wanted so much to belong to them.

"Don't you hate yourself?" one little girl asked maliciously while standing in front of the others.

"Don't you wish you were dead?" another asked.

"Why are your lips so red?" someone asked. "Are you wearing lipstick?"

"Are you a boy, or do you really want to be a girl?"

And so, it went.

Whatever "I" was, it was wrong and bad. The other children "all" knew that. For some reason, even *I* accepted it. I really must be a little pariah. I must *be* something "wrong." My differences stood out too much. And I truly did not belong.

I can see the ugly grimace of contempt conveyed to me by one of the boys who was joining the pack as they closed in on the outcast. Why did they hate me? I always tried to be nice to them. And I simply wanted to belong. In fact, I was kind of a sweet kid. Maybe too sweet. Then it occurred to me. They hated God's Son too. I had learned this, in some way or another, in my experiences at church. So, if I was hated and he was hated, I was in good company. I was now just like him. They hated God's Son, too.

So, Jesus would be my friend!

And in a real way, he became "mine," and I became "his" that day in a way that was palpably real to me.

Christ *Was* There

I know it sounds almost silly that such an event should have such a consequence in my young life. But Christ really was there for me that day. I

24

know it as deeply as I know the sky is blue and the grass is green. And specifically, he wasn't just there for me. He was crying for me and cheering me on. I know this now because of something that happened to me later as an adult.

Years later, as a pastor, I ran across a small pamphlet used as a counseling tool to help victims of abuse find healing. It encouraged these victims to revisit their time of abuse and to ask God where Jesus was during the abuse. I chose to do that one morning in prayer with this incident. I didn't tell my wife what I was doing. In fact, I'm not sure I'd ever told her about this incident. I just wanted to see if what the booklet suggested would work.

I was praying in my office on one side of the house, rehearsing the story with God, and trying to imagine where Jesus might have been. I'm not sure if I was making any headway, but at the same time Becky was praying her daily prayers in a bedroom on the other side of the house. Unexpectedly, she came to find me and knocked at the door of my office where I was praying.

"Jim," she said, urgently, "What's going on?"

"Why do you ask?" I queried.

"I was in prayer just now, and I got the most overwhelming sense of sadness and had tears and compassion for you. I was really weeping with deep-felt sorrow and pity, and I don't know why. I had to come back and tell you."

I knew immediately what it was. Jesus was speaking through her to let me know he truly was there that day, and he was crying for me, too. He *did* draw me close to him. He *did* speak to me on that day. He *did* tell me I would be his friend. And he would be mine, too. He even enabled me to forgive those who had bullied me. After all, that's what Jesus would do:

Forgive one another as God in Christ has forgiven you. (Ephesians 4:32)

And I was able to hear that instruction and accept it. Why? I believe the reason is because my spirit had been awakened by the atmosphere I was raised in as a child in the Greek Orthodox Church. I was raised to be "strong in spirit." And that's to their credit. Despite the cultural layers and the "us vs them" mentality, in the midst of all of the ancient cultic practices of incense and icons, I developed an awareness of the abiding presence of Jesus and a sensitivity to his call.

Chapter 3

STRONG IN SPIRIT:

FAITH FORMATION IN CHILDREN IN MY BIG FAT

GREEK SOUTHERN-FRIED CHURCH

I have described my time in the Worldwide Church of God (WCG) as a season when I was a Christian in a cult. However, I didn't become a Christian *in* the cult.

In the environment of the Greek Orthodox community of Birmingham, Alabama—I call it "My Big Fat Greek Southern-Fried Church"—I had been encountered by Christ all my life, long before I left the faith of my youth to follow the teachings of Herbert W. Armstrong. Even with its cultic issues, the Greek Orthodox church could awaken the spirits of at least some of its little ones. I know it did for me. It can help raise children who are what the book of Luke says John the Baptist came to be: *And the child grew and became* ***strong in spirit***. [emphasis mine] (Luke 1:80).

I'm thankful for the early days of my spiritual formation in the Greek Orthodox Church. It was a faith culture that was taught to us as children, but in many ways, it was something more caught than taught. It happened without my needing to understand one ounce of doctrine, other than that God was holy and Jesus was His Son. We simply served Him because our parents created an atmosphere in which it was understood that that's what humans are simply supposed to do. And as a church rooted in the Early Church Fathers, it conveyed a reverential sense of holiness that has too often been eschewed in our more modern expressions of church.

Technicolor Christianity vs Black and White Christianity

I remember one time giving a report in a comparative religion class at Ambassador College, Big Sandy, Texas in 1977. Big Sandy, along with the mothership campus in Pasadena, California, were the two WCG colleges in the United States. As part of the class, I had to visit a Methodist church.

I reported on my visit. It was an "okay" experience, I said. It was not heavily laced with deep biblical study-sermons like those we received in the Worldwide Church of God services on Sabbaths. This Methodist service was short, methodical (go figure), and kind of lackluster. The service was held in a bland, dated, brick building. I gave an exact report of my boring visit. I was a timid public speaker at the time and refrained as much as possible from eye contact. But I broke the class up with the best line I'd ever used in a speech at college that was quite off the cuff.

"In closing," I concluded, "in some ways, the service was a lot like the service in the Greek church." By that, I was referring to those times in the Greek church that I had found boring and something endured more than enjoyed. But then I added, "Only it was in black and white. The Greek Church is in Technicolor."

The classroom broke up in laughter (you have to remember that this line had more punch in 1977, since it was only in the early 70s that sales of color TVs surpassed black and white). But I spoke the truth. It really is. For all its insistence on being first and foremost Greek and on having the oldest and best liturgy, it is an amazing Technicolor, holy sight, smell, and sound immersive experience that does layer something deep inside you.

Growing Up "Orthodox"

So let me tell you more (from my personal and very subjective experience) about what it was like being raised in the Greek Orthodox Church from Day 1. I can't say that Mama said verbal prayers that I heard in the womb or that any greeting from anyone made me leap in the womb like little John the Baptist did in Luke 1 (unless it was the nervous but kind taxi driver who took Mama to the hospital when she went into labor for my birth). But I know I was raised in a house that paid homage to the holy. And I'm sure I heard a lot of chanting in utero from a very loud, nasal, and usually off-key priest when Mama went to church.

27

In varying and different ways, God was often mentioned. And the concept of holiness and God's ever-watchful presence was made very obvious. We lived in a world where the consciousness of God loomed largely and was spoken of frequently and daily.

"Eine martia to Theo!" Mama would declare with a voice of both mystical and authoritative warning when we were sassy or about to do something wrong. "It's a sin against God!" I can still "feel" the dramatic emphasis on the word "sin" (martia) and the exclamation mark underscoring the inarguable reality of an ever-watchful "God" (Theo) in that phrase. God was holy, therefore we were supposed to be holy. And there were household "sacramental" objects of holiness as well.

For one, bread was holy. If you dropped it on the ground and had to throw it away, you had to kiss it first. I don't know why that was held in such esteem. Perhaps it was because bread represents Jesus' body. I used to think it was because we weren't particularly wealthy and you showed God disdain if you carelessly dropped the bread *He'd* given you on the ground, and you didn't want to dare affront Him. Or maybe it was an even older custom that preceded Christianity. But in our home, if you dropped bread, you kissed it before you threw it away. You did this because God is watching. God is always watching. And even bread is holy.

In our home, there was also a holy place for the holy pictures—the icons. One was of Saint Nicholas, patron saint of Mama's village back home known as Agios Nikolaos. Then there was the one for the Virgin Mary (Panagia) holding the baby Jesus, who looked, by the way, like a very serious and thoughtful four-year-old. And there was one portraying some bearded figure who, to this day, I can't tell you who it was—God the Father perhaps?

But every night you dared not go to bed before you prayed before them. You didn't pray *to* them. You prayed *before* them. That's an important distinction. First, you would say in Greek the Lord's Prayer, which is quite beautiful. Here it is transliterated, with a bit of Greek phrasing, replete with emotion-conveying exclamation points along the way:

Pater hēmōn, ho en tois ouranois

Father of ours, the one in the heavens,

hagiasthētō to onoma sou

Let-be-being-hallowed! the name of-you.

elthetō hē basileia sou

Let-come! the kingdom of you

genethetō to thelēma sou

Let-be-being-become! the will of-you

hōs en ouranōi, kai epi tēs gēs;

As in heaven, also on the earth.

ton arton hēmōn ton epiousion dos hēmin sēmeron

The bread of-us, the dole, be-given! To us today.

kai aphes hēmin ta opheilēmata hēmōn

and remit! to-us the debts of-us

hōs kai hēmeis aphiemen tois opheiletais hēmōn

As also we remit to the debtors of us

kai mē eisenenkēis hēmas eis peirasmon,

And no [sic] you-may-be-bringing-us into testing

alla rhusai hēmas apo tou ponērou.

But rescue-You! us from the hurtful.

Amēn.

I was taught it in Greek and, with the plasticity of a child's mind, I could ape it in Greek. I had no idea what those words meant. But it didn't matter. God was God. And prayer was not an option. You just prayed. Greek parents not only taught children to pray, but they also sometimes even *made* them pray. They weren't worried about contemporary notions of boring their children or turning their children off toward God. Prayer was simply what humans are supposed to do. God gives us life. God gives us everything. God is watching us and is with us all the time. God loves us and protects us all the time. God is the reason you *are*. Prayer was a no-brainer. Your prayer was for God and not for yourself.

It wasn't until years later that I could translate this prayer directly. I can still say it today without even understanding what all the words mean. Its words have stayed with me forever, and believe it or not, they calm my mind when it gets frazzled.

After we said this prayer, our parents taught us to do our cross. By that, I mean to make the sign of the cross. While doing this (the Greek way, of course, unlike the Catholic left-to-right, open-handed way, which to us was akin to swatting flies) we would say:

Agios o Theos

Agios o Hristos

Agios o Pneumato

Eleisonimas.

Roughly translated it means:

Holy is the God

Holy is the Christ

Holy is the Spirit

Have mercy on us.

Next, we would say three times:

Chrestos Christos kepai

Olla kaka skopai

Roughly translated, it means this:

The good the Lord keeps to stay

All of the bad He throws away.

We did this every night, standing piously at the foot of the single bed over whose headframe the icons were assembled. It was a holy spot, and it was a holy time. You didn't go to bed without saying your prayers. You didn't eat without saying your prayers. You did everything with a prayer—or at the very least, silently making the sign of the cross.

There was a sense of God being everywhere. And there was a deep sense of His special presence on Earth. That was the Holy Church. Every Sunday, rain or shine, we were there. We'd drive the 20 minutes from Green Acres to the church in downtown Birmingham. We would go on US 11 through Five

Points West passing The Coffee Cup, a Greek restaurant, and The Hickory Hut, a Greek diner, along the way. You navigated your way through the city by using Greek restaurants, diners, and other holy strongholds or landmarks such as these. We did this every Sunday. That is, all of us except Mama.

Mama had stopped going to church for a while. I'm not sure of all the reasons. Some of us, remembering things she said, think it had something to do with the fact that she hadn't bought a new coat in 15 years and was ashamed to be seen in the same green coat she'd always worn. But Dad, who was also the treasurer and had to go early to get things ready for the offering, made sure three kids and a toddler were up and ready to go to church every Sunday. And he did more than just get us ready physically. He got us ready spiritually and emotionally for the peak day of the week and our peak journey of the week—our ride to go serve God—at church!

It would start on Saturday. We'd go to Uncle Pete's shoeshine and haberdashery store downtown and get our shoes shined—for church. When necessary, we'd get our hair cut—for church. We put on our little suits and our little clip-on ties—for church. Dad would fix pancakes or a special breakfast for Sunday morning—because it was a special day, and he wanted us kids to know it was special. You see we were going somewhere—to church.

And it wasn't just "any" church. It was the one "true" church in town. It was *the* Greek Orthodox Church. Yes, it was downtown, far from our home. But going to where God is truly being worshipped by the most ancient and best-preserved liturgy in the world was worth the drive. Dad did what needed to be done to make church special. And he put God and church first. The two were practically interchangeable to him, and so it was for us.

The Adventure of Going to Church

And what happened at church? Well, amazing things. In the pre-church hours, we had the run of the place while Dad was in the Sunday school building office prepping the offering.

We'd swarm around the basement and the first and second floors of the old brick fellowship hall. On the second floor, there was a stage and a piano. We'd finger out different tunes. I had a good ear, so I learned how to play "Never on Sunday" (of course, a Greek song from the 1960s Jules Dassin movie that helped put Greece back on the contemporary cultural map), while we were waiting to go—to church. We'd walk up and down the halls where the Sunday school rooms were located in our home away from home—church.

Then we'd go to the actual service. Talk about a Technicolor experience! The Greek Orthodox Cathedral in Birmingham is mesmerizing, an amazing work of art with high ceilings and a warmly lit atmosphere. You enter the narthex, the entrance area, where you first light a candle to establish your presence and send up candle-glow prayers to God. You walk through the double doors into the nave, the space where the congregants worshipped, and see beautiful pews, two sections of them, with a long walkway leading up to the altar. Beautiful stained-glass windows surround you and let in the glorious Alabama sun. The altar area where the priest chants the liturgy—the place of *laos ergos* ("people working" for God)—is the place where the brilliantly robed priest leads people serving God, "working" for God, by giving Him their presence and their attention.

Again, it wasn't a "church serve-us," it was a "church serve-God." The priest conducted the liturgy in an open area in front of the richly ornamented half-wall of paintings and icons (the *Iconostasion*) depicting beautiful biblical scenes. I vaguely remember a picture of a very dour-looking man in a desert wearing rough-looking clothes and holding a serving platter with a head on it. This was the head of John the Baptist being held by the resurrected John the Baptist. But he was obviously both Greek and Orthodox and not a Baptist at all. I can't remember the others, except I vaguely remember a white-bearded older man dressed in a robe studded with jewels who was wearing a crown and looking appropriately serious, if not dour. Greeks live life large, but all it takes is a reproving glance from one such icon to put you in your place, for a few moments at least, until you are out of his line of sight.

The half-domed ceiling art that loomed above the elaborately ornate half-wall of wooden arches that divided the altar from where the priest chanted was the "star" of this building's show. Depicted there was the Virgin Mary, arms wide, face pure and loving in an appropriately artistic Byzantine style. She looked like my mother. She looked like all Greek mothers rolled into one ideal one. Above her was a scene of Abraham being visited by the Three Angels (a theophany of the Trinity?) on the way to Sodom. His head is bowed in a position of humility toward the holy visitors as he serves them a meal. His wife Sarah was there, a beautiful woman with heavily lidded Greek eyes, of course, and dressed in Virgin Mary haute couture. She wore a rich red robe that covered her hair. She was serving the holy visitors a meal, too. And oddly enough, it wasn't the freshly killed calf and unleavened bread you read about in Genesis. It was *faki* or lentil soup, or so it seemed. This is a very humble Greek village meal. I always wondered why God was served lentil soup after going to all the trouble of joining Abraham to warn him of the destruction of Sodom. But I guess if you're eating in the Greek church, even God must eat Greek food.

One thing stood out: you were in a holy place. The priest chanted, and the choir sang occasionally and sometimes dramatically, in beautiful mysterious and majestic atonal Byzantine chants. You stood, you sat. You kneeled, you crossed yourself. You heard no English, except when they would pray for the President of the United States (I can still hear the sing-song voice chanting inexplicably in Greek but climaxing with the name "Leen-don-bee Jo-oo-ohn-son!" sung in a bit of an accent no less).

And sometimes, if you were a boy and became extremely bored sitting in church, you could be like little Samuel. You could put on your shiny little altar vestments, tie your sash the proper way, carry a candle, and be in procession with the priest on the "stage" (near the altar). I say "stage" because one time my sister took the little son of a Protestant friend of hers to church with her and thought it necessary to ask him a question during the service. My sister's name is Julia, and he was too young to pronounce it correctly. But he was not too young to make this observation when she distracted him from the service: "Shh, Ju-Ju! I want to watch the show!"

Well, as a little Greek boy, you could be in the show! And do something that was maybe a little hard but holy. You could be an altar boy and hang out in the back and not have to sit through the service. There were perks for serving God. And there was, well, a sense of righteous accomplishment after it that enabled you to kick back and enjoy the "rest" of the day. And "rest" could come only after you served God first. You didn't deserve to rest and enjoy life otherwise. It was just the way life was.

After Church

When church was over, finally over, and you had paid your dues, and maybe it was a lucky day when there was no fifteen minutes of extra prayer for someone who had just passed,* you might get to stand in line and get *andithero* (the leftover communion bread). If you had to tough it out and endure the extra fifteen-minute memorial service for someone who'd recently died, you also got a cracked wheat confection called *koliva*. It was served in little wax bags, and if you were one of the lucky ones, you got one of these with the candy-coated almonds that decorated the powdered sugar mass that formed some kind of cracked wheat and raisin cake in the dead's honor. This was all a part of the memorial services. They didn't occur weekly. But if they did, you were there an extra fifteen minutes after what must have seemed like an interminably long service.

You met people after services to exchange friendly chatter. They'd all been associated with each other since 1906 when the first large influx of Greeks arrived. They kept coming until Birmingham boasted one of the largest Greek communities in the South. When fellowship was finished, we'd get in the car and head to Home Baking Company (Greek-owned, by the way) and get our French bread (made by a Greek, of course) and raisin-bar cookies. And we'd go home to either chicken with lemon and oregano, delicious pot roasts in tomato paste sauces, Greek spaghetti with burnt butter and a crumbly (not soupy) meat sauce seasoned with cinnamon, homemade bread, and "French bread," salad with Greek Kalamata olives, and *real* feta cheese bought from a *real* Greek deli. Maybe with some small green onions, like the ones pictured with the lentil soup the angels and the Lord were served by Abraham and Sarah on the mural at church.

If you missed church because you were too sick to go, Dad determined you'd also be too sick to play that afternoon. Clever man. We were seldom "too sick" to attend church.

What Made Me Strong in Spirit—and Hungry for More

Like John the Baptist, we were gestated, even in the womb, in a culture that at least verbally put God and church (or church and hence God) first. Some of the first sounds I'm sure our developing ears heard while in our mothers' wombs were songs and sounds of the Greek liturgy—the priest chanting at

---

* The Forty-Day Memorial Service held the Sunday after forty days have passed from the death of a loved one. I think there may be an association with the forty-day period Jesus was on Earth until he ascended (Acts 1).

church. Like little Samuels, our parents devoted us to being altar boys dressed in robes appropriate to our size, because we too helped at church, and sometimes, like little Samuel, felt like we lived at church too.

Since Mom was still filled with wonder at the New World, and since her only exposure to it was the wealth and growing financial prosperity of successful and hardworking Greek immigrants, we met people of wonder and achievement at, where else? At church!

We were *in* the American world but not *of* the American world. We belonged to Greece and church and God in that order. We were an amazing culture within a culture. But the culture around me began throwing questions at me about life and community and belonging.

The American kids had cruelly rejected me as a "different" immigrant child. The maturing Greek kids, being part of a commuter church world, didn't provide enough shared life together to create a place of belonging, at least not in those early days when the immigrant culture was still busy getting their feet on the ground with The American Dream.

I began looking for my place in the world. Like Joseph in Genesis 37, I was a teenager beginning to wander in the fields of life looking for *my* brothers. I was looking for them in the context of God. The two seemed to be inextricably connected. I was losing sight of the latter while I still hadn't found the former.

Since the church was so busy with preserving its culture and achieving in the new culture in which it was now immersed, I couldn't know whether God or its people were there for me or not. And either I found the cult, or the cult found me.

Chapter 4

LOOKING FOR MY BROTHERS: THERE'S A LITTLE

"JOSEPH" IN US ALL

s I write this story, I almost feel embarrassed and foolish. I'm writing about simplistic childhood scenes that should not have had the "epic" place in my life that they do. Millions go through similar things and make it through fairly unscathed. They certainly don't earn me an epic sense of pity for all the ways I've viewed these stories. So how did these tiny rudders in a child's life, such mundane childhood events, become such life-changing turns in the course of my life and my world?

Perhaps the strong sense of social isolation we were given by overprotective Greek parents desperate for our "pure" incorporation into a Greek world contributed in part. For what it's worth, second-generation Greek mothers were much more adept at guiding their children into more of a mainstream cultural experience than my first-generation mom (limited I'm sure by some fears and phobias engendered by her World War Two experiences).

But why did these "little" scenes in a very "little" life become such epic, life-changing moments? The answer is simple: because a very big God was indeed part of that little world. And in that context, perhaps all the "little" things of all our "little" lives are truly "epic" to Him, no matter how small they seem to us. For that kind of approach to life, I am not embarrassed. I'm grateful.

The Greeks know how to grow children who are immersed in the sense of the "holy." They know how to grow children who are strong in spirit, and who are trained to hear the call of God. And yet, despite its strengths, I do believe I was positioned for affiliation with the Worldwide Church of God by the "culture within a culture" of my childhood. Hence, in the midst of other teenage struggles that pulled me away from my childhood roots, I gradually found myself moving from one "one true church" to another.

Like Joseph in the Genesis story, I was wandering in the fields of my life, "looking for my brothers" (Genesis 37:16). And like Joseph and all the Israelites would learn, you've sometimes got to go to Egypt before you get to the Promised Land.

Growing Up Greek in Green Acres

Green Acres was a fun, middle-class, blue-collar neighborhood. All the houses in the section where I lived were modest and inexpensive, with part brick and part wooden siding. They were not ostentatious. They were bounded by one neighborhood of larger, better-quality homes on their west end and smaller older homes on their east end. All the ones in my section were built in the fifties, and all our World War Two veteran dads moved us into them at the same time. We had our own elementary school. Green Acres Elementary brought us through grades one to eight, so we all went through early childhood, puberty, and adolescence together. We had our own Boy Scout Troop. We had our own little grocery store called the Dixie Supermarket. And we had our own little candy store named Baker's, about as big as a postage stamp, where a friendly lady named Mrs. Baker would sell the kids candy, and sometimes cigarettes, with a grandmotherly air. It was as homey an American post-war community as you'd ever find.

It was homey, but we were made aware in many ways that it was not *our* home. We were only one of two Greek families in the neighborhood, and even while part of the above environment, we maintained a fairly insular life. We marked our life maps by other bastions of Greek occupation in the city, as we would drive to God's one true church every Sunday. We lived in a superior "Greek world" within the wider (albeit inferior) "American world" of Green Acres.

We looked very much the large-eyed children of our Greek immigrant mom. I wore my brother's hand-me-downs, and since he was always head and shoulders taller than everyone, my belt was always tied right below my rib cage and covered by bulky warm sweaters. We were smart and at the top of our class in school, like all good second and third-generation immigrant children are supposed to be.

I remember being on my own a lot. But I also remember, on my best days, being content. After the episode of social rejection at grammar school, I was securely aware of one thing in a very personal way: I really did belong to Jesus. I *was* Christ's. He and I were really tight. He loved me, I loved him. He forgave us, I forgave those people who hated me, too. I guess the statement is true: big God, little trial. So, I didn't have an inordinate sense of needing to grieve. I had Jesus, so what I was missing was pale by comparison. I felt like we were on a mission together. This relationship with Jesus was palpably real and sustained me, frankly, much the same way it does today. But the elements of life were appropriate to my age.

For example, as I grew older, I became more culturally aware of the life options available to me in the land of opportunity. We knew more about American life than Mom did. And I wanted more, in particular, more status and belonging in the non-Greek world in which I found myself. I wanted association in their world and a sense of belonging and significance and success. I began looking for my flesh and blood brothers on Earth, the audience before whom to play out the drama of my life. And with immigrant persistence and perseverance, I finally figured out who could help me find them. It was the one who had become my best Friend in the first place: Jesus Christ. He began to teach me how to pray differently.

It was the summer after the fifth grade that I personally broke The Prayer Barrier. That year had been particularly difficult socially. I remember going through whole days just trying to see if I could get away without saying one word in school. I was still the social outcast. I felt like even the teacher was laughing at me. I wanted more. So, I began *praying* prayers instead of *saying* prayers. And that changed everything.

No Longer "Saying" Prayers but "Praying" Prayers

I started to *ask* God for specific things. Instead of just saying the same recited words (which, I would like to say, I don't think is necessarily always bad), I started asking for things I knew were good to have, and things that I knew I wanted. Facing the truth that we were out-of-step immigrant kids, I wanted to be a regular American boy. I wanted to fit in. I wanted to belong. Like Pinocchio, I wanted to be a "real boy." I prayed for that regularly that summer.

I didn't believe that the reason I didn't belong was just that "they" were mean to me. I believed there were things I could be and do better. And I began asking God for help with that. I began praying prayers instead of just saying prayers. And guess what? God answered.

I went from being the big-eyed, buzz-headed immigrant boy Jimmie (named, embarrassingly, after the leader of the Mickey Mouse Club who spelled his name with an "ie") to the more masculine and cooler Jim. And this "Jim" was a surprise to many. Kids who knew me in the earlier grades didn't recognize the sixth-grade Jim. The new Jim was popular with a vengeance. A Beatles haircut was just the right touch for my big-eyed triangular little Eastern European face. The girls thought I was cute. The guys thought I was smart and funny. I began to belong. And I knew where that belonging came from.

Although God's goal is not to move us from the outcast to the popular crowd (sometimes quite the opposite!) in the rawness of my experience with Christ I believe God answered that prayer. It was a direct answer to a direct and specific request. I had no doubt it came from God.

I'd also asked to be witty and humorous like my mom could be, and guess what? Suddenly, I was quite the comedian in class. I could make people laugh! I could even make the teacher laugh. By the eighth grade, I could occasionally stop the class with witty responses and questions that were just too engaging to avoid. I'm sure in one sense God was beginning to develop the crowd communication skills He would later use in me as a Bible teacher and evangelist. But I knew— and *knew* that I knew—that this newfound status in social life and persona came directly from God. I wasn't who I was before. Something had changed.

And I was very soon going to hear my version of God's "Samuel Call" (1 Samuel 3) to me.

God Becoming My Personal God

Life was getting better. God did answer prayer, and I truly, truly believed that He was with me. It was an honest-to-God life transformation; it was an experiential miracle. I know this sounds childish and almost like a fairy tale, but to the very roots of my being, I know this really happened. God was real. And He could make things happen for someone like me in a real way.

I felt a keen awareness of God's sovereign work in my life. Even when the flow of my popularity ebbed, I sensed it was because he was nudging me to want something more than just social acceptance and popularity. He wanted me to constantly need and want *Him*. He wanted me to be in a constant state of personal engagement with Him. And with my deepening sense of intimacy with God, my prayer life evolved some more.

My friends and I were maturing and entering adolescence. We were ready to step into the big leagues of our teenage years and were forming new alliances daily. There were no particular bright spots or dark spots for that period that I remember, but there was one situation that would become a bit of a constant in my life through the end of my high school years.

In the name of Jesus, I would become a human crutch. I did so to join Jesus in a life of service—even if it meant serving those who had been "mean" to me.

Joining Jesus in a Life of Service

It was sometimes during that time that I decided to help a boy named Billy by carrying his books. He had a rare condition called Friedrich's Ataxia. It caused him to lose his ability to walk unaided and to carry his own books between classes. For several of the next seven years, until we both graduated from high school, he would place his hand on my shoulder between classes and I became his human crutch and book carrier. Arms extended to my thighs, I'd sometimes carry as many as ten hardbound schoolbooks—his and mine—at the same time. It was quite a workout. I fulfilled this role until his muscular deterioration had gotten so bad that I ended up pushing him around in his wheelchair from room to room as necessary. Bill, as he came later to be called, is in Heaven now.

For what it's worth, Billy had been among the ring leaders of the kids who'd surrounded me when I was little and asked why I didn't hate myself. He was the one who gave me the most memorable scowl of contempt and rejection that I wrote about earlier.

But my best friend Jesus forgave and served with his life. So, I tried to do the same. I wanted to emulate Jesus, my brother and best friend. And so I guess I shouldn't have been surprised when I actually became a blessing to Billy and his family, and he was one to me, too.

In Billy, I had at least one brother to belong to. Things continued a fairly even, if not boring, keel until something happened during the summer before my eighth-grade year that threw me for a loop. I ran across the cover of *Time Magazine* asking the question "Is God Dead?"

It stopped me in my tracks. I never thought about the possibility that God might not exist. And it threw me not only for a loop, but for a horrifying loop. What if God really wasn't there? Or worse yet, in a spirit of true

Byzantine terror, what if you got deceived into believing He wasn't there, and He really was there? Either Hell on Earth or Hell in the afterlife (or both!) yawned before me.

Neither option was a soul-nourishing place to be for someone just entering the eighth grade.

A Holy Horror—a World Without God

It was a holy horror—the possibility of a world without God. Could that possibly be true? Could God truly be dead or never there at all? That can't be! It would be unbearable if it was true.

God was the One who saved me from loneliness, from grueling social isolation. God was the One who comforted me when the kids cruelly rejected me. God was the one who made me popular, transformed me, and gave me something to do and someone to be. God was the one who was with me when I was down, who'd be with me when Mom and Dad were no longer around.

God was my hope for everything. If *He* wasn't there, then I was truly on my own, at the mercy of all the beast-like "dog eat dog" cruelty that there is in the world. Friends and a sense of belonging were inching away again—a sort of adolescent depression was setting in—all because an awful possibility had been introduced to me.

The Enemy took an inch and made it a mile. Smart people were now saying God might not exist! It was a holy horror to have to live in this cruel world without God. Who was going to be able to help me now? If God was dead, then how would I face this world?

The Dark Night of an Adolescent Greek Soul and Crisis in Birmingham

A period of incredible sadness set in. I don't think it was clinical depression, but it was a sad period in my life. This world was too scary for me to face alone. Mama noticed and would kindly ask me if I was okay. Yet I didn't know how to talk about these things. How could I even begin to admit to anybody I was afraid God wasn't there? That sounded blasphemous. And besides, God had to be there! But who could help me find Him?

I finally talked to Dad, and he suggested the priest at the church, so I do remember speaking to him. We had a very brief and not very impactful conversation. In hindsight, I now realize that perhaps the priest and the whole church may have been preoccupied at the time by a major cultural shift taking place in this deep South city at the time. I had no idea this was going on until just recently.

I don't have dates or facts or figures, but in the 1960s, when I was going through all this spiritual angst, the Greek Church in Birmingham was going through a cultural crisis of its own. Or so says author Andrew Manis, who has chronicled this in an article published in the Department of American Studies at Aristotle University of Thessaloniki, Greece.[3] The priest present at the time had bravely decided (along with some other local pastors) to support the cause of Dr. Martin Luther King, Jr. Dr. King's efforts to bring dignity and equality to blacks in the Deep South, and particularly in Birmingham, are now the stuff of legend. I'm so proud to learn that my priest fought on that side.

As is well documented, there was resistance from some of the white clergy in Birmingham against Dr. King (of which King speaks boldly about in his "Letter from the Birmingham Jail"). However, our priest, Father Sam Gouvelis, bravely joined other American pastors in writing a letter of support for him. This support for black Americans by the Greek Orthodox Church went as far as Archbishop Iakovos, who himself got involved. He marched with Dr. King from Selma, and a photograph of that march made the cover of *Life Magazine* in March of 1965.

Although no one I've talked to remembers this, and I personally don't, Dr. Manis writes that there was some resistance to this support of Dr. King *within our very own Birmingham congregation*. Some Greek business owners, becoming increasingly successful, feared that such an association might hurt their businesses. They feared that some Alabama "whites" might stop doing business with them if they were too visibly supportive of Dr. King's agenda.

Although I know we all were impacted by, and guilty of, at least some of the embedded racism of the day, I for one don't remember my parents being anything but positive in their attitude about Dr. King's movement and the cause of civil rights. I know my uncle personally stood up for his black employees, refusing requests to not let them share a ride in his truck when some white employees complained. "They're just as good as you," he said. Mama always went out of her way to show her black associates special compassion, because she was compassionate for the underdog and savvy enough to recognize that they deserved to be honored the way all children of God should be honored.

This was going on during the time I was growing up in the church and was having such deep questions about God, and may have unconsciously contributed to my existential angst. My Greek brothers and sisters are the most loving people I know. I believe they have some of the richest, purest doctrine in modern-day Christianity.

Why then did all that wonderful doctrine seem so unavailable to me when I needed it most? When I, as a 14-year-old confused and scared kid, was desperately looking for someone to prove to me there was a God, neither the priest nor the church was present enough to be able to give me a meaningful sense of belonging or an answer. My Protestant friends never talked as if they knew Jesus or shared anything about him. But I had to know. Did God really exist? Was the Bible true? Could someone reassure me and give me God back, and fill this aching hole I felt inside?

"The World Tomorrow" Broadcast Reached My Young Ears

Here's what happened next. One evening that fall we were driving home (I can't remember from where) and I was in the back seat of our white 1965 Dodge Coronet 440. We pulled into our parking space, braking right in front of our sloping driveway, and no one seemed to be listening to the radio except me. It was at that very minute, as the sun was setting, that I heard a voice on the airwaves announcing two free booklets. "Does God Exist?" was one of them. And the second was "The Proof of the Bible."

It caught my attention. The broadcast was called "The World Tomorrow." You could pick it up almost anywhere. The voice belonged to Herbert Armstrong, the founder of a Pasadena, California-based church, that was then the very global Worldwide Church of God.

I wrote to request the booklets. I devoured them as soon as they came. They made sense. They gave me hope. They put my nose in the Bible in a personal way that engaged me not just with Scriptural reasoning but with a sense of God's presence. I can't explain that, but I began to *feel* God again. God was in His heaven! So, all was once again "right" with my world.

I wrote away for more booklets that cleverly posed the questions I was asking of life. They gave biblical answers that seemed—and felt—plausible. These people did what my Orthodox brothers couldn't. They gave a sense of God back to me. After that, they could do no wrong. I was sold on joining them.

Wherever we were coming home from that night, that trip took me on a detour in my search for God and my brothers that would take a full 40 years to complete. It became my journey with The Worldwide Church of God and its descendant, Grace Communion International.

I was a Christian. But I was also very much going to be a Christian in a cult—a real live cult in the pejorative sense. A cult that would make the list in the books about heretical cults (e.g., The *Kingdom of the Cults*, by Walter R. Martin, featuring WCG along with Mormonism, Jehovah's Witness, Christian Scientist, the Bahai, Hare Krishna, Zen Buddhism, etc.).[4]

As an adolescent in the Greek Orthodox world, I was like Joseph in the book of Genesis, looking for my brothers. Entering WCG felt like my Exodus experience at the time. It would be followed by a very "book-of-Leviticus" phase of my life where I would learn and live many of the laws of the book of Leviticus. I would "wander" in that spiritual desert (and at the same time oasis) for forty years, just like the Israelites did in the book of Numbers. And it's amazing how well this forty-year wandering worked for me. I was heading to the promised land, but unbeknownst to me, I was still living under a slavery, this time a slavery to the slavery of the law, in a Leviticus-like legalism from which I would eventually have to be thrust out.

Perhaps you're going in circles for "Numbers" of years. Or maybe you're with the fulfillment of Joshua (Jesus) just on the border of recognizing the real Promised Land, the Kingdom of Heaven, which is nearer than you know!

Let me give you a window into my WCG experience. It was a place of great blessing. And it was also a place of bondage.

I was going to be a very profound Christian. But I was going to be a Christian in a cult.

Chapter 5

THE WORLDWIDE

CHURCH OF GOD

T he Worldwide Church of God was founded by Herbert W. Armstrong in 1933 in Oregon, and in its heyday was headquartered in Pasadena, California.

It was always a small denomination, at one time reaching a peak membership of at least 140,000 people worldwide. But WCG was not small in scope or impact or in its ability to communicate with inquiring minds. Its flagship magazine, *The Plain Truth*, had a circulation of over eight million at one point. Its radio broadcast and later its television program, "The World Tomorrow," were estimated to have reached millions. In 1994, the denomination numbered 120,000 people in attendance every week and had an annual income of 200 million dollars. The Ambassador Auditorium at the church's headquarters facilities and main college campus in Pasadena, California was well known by many for its magnificent architectural and acoustic design, playing host to celebrities such as Bing Crosby and Arthur Rubenstein. The denomination's founder, Herbert W. Armstrong, and his son, Garner Ted, were nationally recognized as well. Here is how it all began.

A Sabbath Centerpiece

Herbert W. Armstrong was born into a Quaker family in Des Moines, Iowa in 1892 but did not begin to see himself as an actively religious man until the mid-1920s. He had worked primarily in the advertising business, selling laundry soap among other things. After years of financial successes and failures, he "was 'goaded' by his wife's 'religious fanaticism' that had come through her association with a Seventh–Day Adventist woman who had convinced her it was a sin against God to worship on Sunday rather than

Saturday."[5] Threatening his wife with divorce for this "fanaticism" as he saw it, and placing his whole religious focus on which day Christians were supposed to worship, he offered this challenge:

> "I will give you just one more chance before we separate and get a divorce," I said. "I don't know just where it is, but I know all these churches can't be wrong! I know it's in the Bible that we are to keep Sunday . . . I'll find where the Bible commands us to observe Sunday. I'll prove it to you out of the Bible![6]

After a period of intensive self-study beginning in the fall of 1926, he became convinced that "the six-day creation with a seventh day of rest" was indeed "the key to understanding worship for the church."[7] After a 1927 baptism, he began a search for the "true" church, "convinced that only congregations worshiping on the seventh day qualified."[8] After a series of associations and broken associations with various Seventh-Day churches, he began an independent ministry that expanded into a national radio ministry that would eventually include the publication of *The Plain Truth* magazine to go along with the hundreds of worshipping congregations.

Acknowledging Armstrong's variance with orthodoxy, religious researcher Ruth Tucker writes that for "Armstrong, it became the ultimate test of faith . . . true faith could not be demonstrated unless the Sabbath was maintained."[9] In this passage, Tucker reports of an incident where Armstrong refused to pray for the healing of a crippled man because he was "unwilling to obey God and comply with God's written conditions for healing which included 'keeping God's commandments and believing.'" When it came to commandments, Armstrong meant "particularly . . . God's Sabbath." Since this man and his wife were unwilling to comply in that area, Armstrong "could not pray for him."[10]

Not only was healing, or the lack thereof, associated with Sabbath-keeping, but also his doctrine of salvation and sin. "Satan's first effort was to persuade Adam and Eve to switch from the seventh-day Sabbath to the first day of the week," Tucker noted, quoting Armstrong.[11] Sin, it seemed, stemmed originally from an effort to deceive humanity about the true day of worship. Sabbath-breaking was to be viewed as such a serious matter in Armstrong's theology that it was eventually seen to result in condemnation in the lake of fire.[12]

Considering the primal importance of the Sabbath day, other conventionally accepted understandings in mainstream (and indeed historical) Christianity came under suspicion and eventually revision. Tucker explained that "tied very closely to his insistence on keeping the Sabbath" became Armstrong's "dogmatic assertion that Jesus rose from the dead on Saturday rather than on Sunday." "He argued that Jesus was not crucified on Friday, as had been generally assumed, but on Wednesday, and that he was for three full days and nights in the tomb." Tucker acknowledges that this was not an original proposition by Armstrong, but argues that "he, more than others, sought to correlate the claim with his views on the Sabbath."[13]

"Correlation" is what I would argue is the critical term. Armstrong did not begin to study the subject of the day of the Resurrection until the late summer of 1927, well after he became convinced of the foundational importance of the truth about the Sabbath. It is my opinion, after years of being a member of the fellowship both before and after its doctrinal changes, that this altering of the traditionally accepted version of the Christ story was done to reinforce the supremacy of the seventh-day Sabbath. By this time, Armstrong was so convinced about the truth of the Sabbath, that it became a foundational axiom and began to shape the way other parts of the Bible and salvation story were read and understood. "With the Sunday resurrection illusion shattered, the last supposed [sic] foundation for Sunday observance had been shattered."[14] And an eclectic, decidedly counter-cultural approach to doctrinal development was coincidentally reinforced.

Armstrong's Doctrinal Development

Again, while there were many less central teachings, everything in WCG seemed to stem from the experiences associated with discovering the "true" Sabbath. For Armstrong, this was the biggest and most graphic "us vs them" reference point, for it consigned those who disagreed to the worst of fates. They were often referred to as "so-called Christians" and their churches were considered watered-down versions of the real thing, and occasionally as "churches of the devil."

In addition to the weekly Sabbath, the Worldwide Church of God observed seven annual Sabbaths based on Leviticus 23. These also became non-negotiable "givens" in their doctrinal formulation. Having become "givens," interpretations regarding how these days revealed God's Master Plan of

Salvation were attached, primarily related to Armstrong's unique explanation of biblical prophecy.

The "right" ritual (Sabbath and Holy Day observance), anti-orthodoxy, and a sincere but untrained reliance on the Bible had become our "story." It led to a unique and patently non-orthodox version of the salvation story, at least from the evangelical perspective with which they would eventually align themselves.

A doctrine that began with an unshakeable conviction about the seventh day and the seven Levitical festival days eventually led to other "doctrinal emphases" that hallmarked our belief system (according to author Joseph Tkach, Jr.):[15]

- A doctrine of God that saw Him as both "eternal, immutable, and sovereign" but also "constantly learning and growing." He was seen as having eyes, ears, a nose, lips, and other body parts. In this non-Trinitarian framework, the deity of Christ was somehow upheld, even though he was of a lesser "rank" than God the Father. The Holy Spirit was seen as neither a "ghost" nor a "person" but as "the power of God," called an "it" and not a "He." The primary mission of Jesus was to prove that the Law (which, incidentally, contained the "lost truth" about the Sabbath days) could and should be kept. The quest of every believer was to become part of the "God family," as Armstrong so often put it, and to eventually grow up as sons and daughters of God. Indeed, members freely quoted a teaching that was foundational in the WCG culture—humanity was "to become God even as God is God."

- A unique doctrine of humanity in which it was taught that God was "literally reproducing himself through mankind [sic]."

- A view of salvation that said that those who believed in Jesus Christ and committed themselves to keep the law (the law God gave to Israel through Moses) would become "begotten" (which the Worldwide Church of God understood as meaning "conceived") children of God waiting to be "born again" at the resurrection. Hence, no one was really "saved" in his or her earthly life. We believed "begotten" humans were just impregnated with the potential of salvation. Final delivery would occur only when we as "the begotten" completed the overcoming process attached to salvation. This overcoming process again included obedience to many Old Covenant customs, including Sabbath days and festival days commanded in Leviticus 23.

- Denunciation of Roman Catholicism as "the Great Whore" of Scripture, mainstream Protestantism as her "harlot daughters," and the Worldwide Church of God as "the only one true church in the world." The church did not see itself as either stemming from Catholicism or Protestantism but stemming directly from the work of Jesus Christ and the New Testament church. In its thinking, Protestantism had fallen into "harlotry" because it had accepted the deceptions floating around negating the Sabbath and God's true festival days.

- A view of the world that taught a unique version of British-Israelism (claiming that all Anglo-Saxons were the descendants of the Lost Ten Tribes of Israel and hence required to be Sabbath-keepers) and of church history (claiming that the Worldwide Church of God traced its roots back to the New Testament and through obscure sects throughout history that valiantly preserved the truth of Sabbath-keeping). This view further distinguished WCG from the Seventh-Day Adventists, who refused to hold to British Israelism.

- An eschatological view that upheld a literal view of the millennium and three separate resurrections. One would be for the resurrected saints from this "smaller" first harvest of the church (of "true Sabbath-keepers") that would rise to meet the Lord in the air at his coming and rule with him (on a Kingdom-conquered Earth) as part of the God Family in the millennial kingdom. A second would be for those who had not heard "the Truth" (about the Sabbath, festival days, etc.) in their earthly lifetimes and would be given a chance to have the saints teach them correct doctrine. A third would be the resurrection of all willful sinners from the dead, to be thrown into the lake of fire where they would perish and cease for eternity, with no consciousness whatever.

- Finally, a view of the Old Covenant that only acknowledged the abolition of animal sacrifices and circumcision and required a multitude of Old Testament practices in the church, including its stance toward worship days.

"Behold, how great a matter a little fire kindleth." (James 3:5)

49

Looking back in hindsight, many of us are amazed at the sprawling doctrine that Armstrong developed from the "little fire" of attaching so much importance to the keeping of the Sabbath and of the other biblical days.

Keeping the Days

Originally, Armstrong did not understand that the biblical festival days were to be kept as well as the seventh-day Sabbath. But eventually, he began to see that "the weekly Sabbath and the annual Sabbaths stand or fall together. The arguments used against the annual Sabbaths will be the identical arguments used to overthrow the Sabbath—and if these arguments could hold, then they would abolish the weekly Sabbath!"[16]

Since it was impossible by now for the Sabbath to be abolished in this cultic system, the Levitical Sabbaths (we called them God's "Holy Days") had to be accepted. As a narrative framework for the rituals, Armstrong attached the following meanings to the days—meanings that shaped generations of people's views about the salvation story, both past, present, and future. The salvation "story," compressed through the lens of these days, as I understood and taught them, were as follows:

1) The Passover, in early spring, pictured the death of Christ, the Lamb of God, who came to take away the sin of the world. It also pictured the saving act of God that facilitated our "exodus" from the spiritual Egypt of this world's false system, religious and otherwise.

2) The Festival of Unleavened Bread that immediately followed the Passover, taught us the importance of putting the "leaven" of sin out of our lives. We would picture this lesson by literally searching for and putting away all leavening and leavened products (including bread, cracker, and cookie crumbs that had accumulated in our homes, offices, and cars during the year) and for the seven days of this festival, eat no leavened products.

3) The Day of Pentecost, pictured both the founding of the New Testament church and the giving of the Ten Commandments at Mount Sinai.

4) The Feast of Trumpets pictured the Second Coming of Christ to rule all nations in power and glory, and was correlated with the Seven Trumpets mentioned in the book of Revelation.

5) The Day of Atonement (kept with a required fast) pictured the true instigator of all sin, Satan, being put away forever.

6) The week-long Feast of Tabernacles pictured the coming Millennium, the literal thousand-year reign of the Kingdom of God under the rule of Christ and the finally born again (no longer just "begotten") children of God.

7) The Eighth Day of the Feast,* (the last special "Sabbath" that immediately followed the seven-day Feast of Tabernacles), pictured the time when all the unsaved dead (the majority of humanity who had not learned the "truth" about the Sabbath and the Holy Days) would be resurrected physically and be given a chance to learn these truths at a time when they would have ideal conditions that would enable them to "accept them" and thus be saved.

Armstrong was not totally arbitrary in his attaching of "meaning" to these worship days. Many of his findings bear similarities with scenarios depicted in various other commentaries and writings. Author John Hagee saw them as having great prophetic significance and tied them to a divine seven-thousand-year plan for mankind.[17] But Armstrong's eclectic mix was different, because both ritual and anti-orthodoxy had been primal elements of our story. Thankfully, so was a commitment to ongoing biblical study and ongoing biblical responsiveness. It was this commitment that would help facilitate a total collapse of most of Armstrong's worldview, which indeed had become "worldwide" since its humble beginnings during the Depression era.

No Shortage of Success

From its small beginnings, Armstrong's initial ministry had gradually grown along the Pacific Coast of the United States. In 1947, he moved the ministry to Pasadena, California where he began the first of what would eventually become three campuses of Ambassador College. At the colleges, he began to train leaders for the church.

---

* Also known as "The Last Great Day" referenced above. I believe it embedded a cultural predisposition (and in some cases, preferred lifestyle approach) to leave evangelism to God and "the future." How distorted are our theological lenses even after our changes? For all that we later decried about Armstrong's teaching after our doctrinal "reformation," we would be wise to consider how influenced we are by its underlying effects. Doctrines change much sooner than less conscious cultic tendencies.

As these leaders were sent out, the church grew rapidly in the 1950s and the 1960s. Radio ministries (accounting for the original name of the fellowship, the Radio Church of God) began in other nations, eventually leading to the growth of the church in Canada, Europe, England, Australia, the Philippines, Latin America, and Africa. The church then changed its name to the Worldwide Church of God during this period. A main focus of these radio ministries was prophecy-based messages dealing with the impending second coming of Christ, with various dates (1975 in particular) being speculated as the time of his return.

One of the key personalities and leaders during these years was Armstrong's controversial son, Garner Ted Armstrong. Eloquent, handsome, and charismatic, he became a nationally known radio and television personality in his own right, even being invited to appear on a popular national television variety show (*Hee Haw*, no less) in the 1970s. Growth was significant during the 1950s and 1960s but began to slow in the 1970s. Christ had not returned, minor doctrines had been changed, and the younger Armstrong became embroiled in various allegations of moral misconduct.

Still, the church continued to hold its own, reaching the status and size described earlier during the years following its founder's death in 1986 and continuing to provide a place of spiritual community, belonging, and understanding of the world for many.

I was one of them.

At an early age, they, not the Greek Orthodox Church, gave God back to me.

Chapter 6

1 CAME TO GOD—NOT

A CULT: AND HE CAME TO ME

Make no mistake.

When I joined WCG, I did it for God.

I didn't just join a cult.

What I did, I did for God.

I came to God.

And so did the many thousands of wonderful people who also "bought in" to Herbert Armstrong's teachings.

The doctrine was wrong. But the people who I knew in my Worldwide journey were "salt of the earth" folks. *A desire to love God with all your heart and soul and mind and strength is never wrong. And a willingness to live that out is not wrong either.* And that's what so many in this group did in so many ways. They were as sincere and dedicated as any disciples you'll find in Christendom. It would be wrong to focus on what was wrong about them more than what was honorable and *of Christ in* them.

Even if I and others in WCG wandered in the wilderness for forty years, I believe that God was with us every step of the way. I believe this just like I believe God has been with *you* every step of your way in whatever cultic paradigms you've been trapped in. Because we are all victims of our own cultural preferences and prejudices, *whether we realize it or not.* And I believe that because we are all created in Christ (Ephesians 2:10), and we are always in Christ (Colossians 1:17), he is the Truth even of what we are (John 14:6). That means he has always been with us, *whether we realize it or not.*

In the last chapter, we focused on Armstrong's history and doctrine. Bear with me in this chapter as I attempt to give you my best picture of our lives in Armstrong's world. There is some regret in retracing these steps. But there is gratitude as well. Christ did so many amazing things for me and others while we were on that leg of our journey. And I will forever be honored to have shared that journey with so many wonderful people. It was a cult, but in spite of all the counterfeit, there was something real that drew us in. We came to God.

And He knows that.

I Came to God

So, there I was, in the back seat of our family car and rolling into our parking space at home on that momentous night. The dark of the evening was beginning to fall sometime in the autumn of 1968. I heard Herbert Armstrong's voice crackling over the radio. I heard him offering these two booklets that I hoped had the answers I was so desperately looking for. "Does God Exist?" was one of them. "The Proof of the Bible" was the second one. To top it all off, they were free. I memorized the address and wrote for them. Soon, they were delivered to my family's door.

I'm sure my father had no idea of the doctrinal and cultural Pandora's Box that was being delivered to his mailbox. Whatever else Dad was, he always granted us our right to choose, explore, reach out, and grow.

To this date, my only rebellion against the family's cultural norm had been to insist on a Beatles haircut rather than a regular boy's haircut. Other than that, I'd been a pretty cooperative young adolescent. I did have a passion for all things historically Greek. It had become part of my self-definition, part of what gave me a special identity. And I loved stories of Mama's family in Greece, told with such a glow in her eyes. Her heart was still there. In my heart I was a loving and loyal patron of the culture. It was who I was too.

But *I had to know* whether God was there or not. He was the One who comforted me when I was such a small kid, rejected so cruelly and having no one else to turn to. He was the One who answered my prayers in the fifth grade, the One who gave me a life and a place to belong. He just had to be there!

I began to see that the status symbols of life were shifting and passing. But if He was there, you could always weather any storm. Those booklets proved to me that He was there! It was one of the most affirming periods of my life. With surety, I could again believe that God did exist and that the Bible was true.

How Did They Prove God to Me?

Here's what I remember learning and what I began to understand. The logic from the booklets was not necessarily overly profound nor theologically precise. But it was compelling, fascinating, and comprehensible. It convinced me there was truly "proof" that God existed, and His word was true.

My desire happened to be a good one: I wanted knowledge-based proof that God existed. And the amazing communication skills of this group of people did the trick. Looking back, I see the mastery of Armstrong and other WCG teachers in cobbling disconnected Scriptures together to prove a point that we wanted to be true. Their teaching was wrong, but the result felt "right." I ended up with a palpable sense of God's presence and with a profound belief in the Bible.

Especially impactful was my introduction to biblical prophecy. God predicting the relevant future in the distant past was especially impactful for me. The lynchpin came in a booklet I ordered called "The United States and British Commonwealth in Prophecy," written by Armstrong. It posited that the Lost Ten Tribes of Israel wandered through Europe through the centuries until two of them destined for international greatness miraculously made it to Great Britain. From there, the obvious "truth" was that the promises of international greatness given in the Scriptures to the descendants of Ancient Israel, and in particular the tribes of Ephraim and Manasseh, had never been fulfilled in ancient times.

And if God was true, these prophecies just "had" to be fulfilled, in some big, global, historically relevant (and for us, some twentieth-century) way. They were fulfilled, the reasoning added, but only when the United States and Britain fulfilled them. The United States was "proven" to be descended from the tribe of Manasseh. Great Britain was assumed to be descended from Ephraim. And you could deduce this by understanding ancient prophecies in the "true" way they were "really" written, overlooked by the world for centuries. It focused on a detailed study of the promises made to the patriarch Abraham and then refined with specificity for his grandson Jacob, then passed down by Jacob to Ephraim and Manasseh, the sons of his favorite son Joseph, in a special blessing given in Genesis 48.

In Kings James English, I read for myself where Jacob was told, *And God said unto him, I am God Almighty: be fruitful and multiply;* **a nation** *and a* **company** *of nations shall be of thee, and kings shall come out of thy loins.* [emphasis mine] (Genesis 35:11, KJV)*

Somehow, somewhere a "company" of nations was morphed to mean "a commonwealth of nations." Wasn't the British Empire eventually also called the British *Commonwealth*? To my biblically inexperienced mind, that was astounding.

And wasn't the United States, emerging from its British mother country (or "brother" country, as we saw it, since we saw them as the descendants of brothers Manasseh and Ephraim), the single greatest nation of all history, and hence had to be the global fulfillment of this prophecy?

Hmmm . . . *a nation and a* **company** *of nations shall be of thee, and kings shall come out of thy loins* [emphasis mine] (Genesis 35:11, KJV). This was sounding more and more interesting.

"A nation" of God-touched greatness---the United States, I began to see. "And a company" ----or *commonwealth*---"of nations!" Great Britain, it seemed obvious to me. A teaching about biblical "time cycles" intrigued me as well.

It was proven to me! The Bible's prophecies came true! God was real! They gave God back to me! And from that point on, they could teach no wrong. I was once again a sincere Christian with hope. I was also a Christian in an official cult.

There was to be only one response now: to give back everything to Him. I didn't want to lose Him ever again. Life was too empty without Him. There

---

* In Genesis 48:19 (KJV), Jacob supposedly transferred these specific promises of "a nation and a company of nations" to the sons of Joseph when blessing them, saying: "he (Manasseh) also shall become a people, and he also shall be great: but truly his younger brother (Ephraim) shall be greater than he, and his seed shall become a multitude of nations." That was viewed by Armstrong to be the transmission of the blessing given in Genesis 35:11 above to Ephraim (viewed to be the tribe that became Great Britain who was seen as a "multitude" or "company" or commonwealth of nations) and to Manasseh (viewed to be the tribe that became the United States, a people or nation who were "truly great"). Again, I no longer hold to this. My intent is to illustrate how fascinatingly "plausible" assumptions can be strung together to "unearth" some "hidden" truth to an American culture today that still has a penchant for dramatic conspiracy theories. There truly is nothing new under the "Conspiracy Theory" sun.

was only one choice: follow Him with all my being from this point on. I couldn't face this cold world alone. Now I didn't have to.

Giving It All Up—For God

So, they'd given God back to me and, in the months that followed shortly thereafter, God had given me my social standing back at school and among my peers. God had to be in all of this. If God was supposed to be *first*, then first must really mean *first*.

Or so I reasoned. I wasn't going to risk losing sight of Him again. So, I had to respond, and I guess I did. Below are points of how I did this over the next 20 years:

- At the age of 15, I was given the courage to tell my parents I was no longer attending the Greek Orthodox Church. It broke their hearts. In hindsight, it broke mine, too. But Daddy understood. He allowed it because he knew I truly believed that I was following God. It took a tremendous amount of initiative and courage to do so, and it happened in ways only God could have made happen. God was with me, even though I was joining a "cult."
- I found my way to begin attending the local congregation of the Birmingham Worldwide Church of God.
- I applied and was accepted to Ambassador College in Big Sandy Texas, one of their three Bible colleges (one in Pasadena, California, one in Big Sandy, and one in St. Albans, England). Like many of my Greek forebears who came to this country with a sincere faith in God, I still remember reading Genesis 12 as we journeyed to Big Sandy in my family's car. It was one of the first experiences with Scripture where I just *knew* God was speaking to me. To this day, I believe He was directing my attention to this verse:

    Go from your country, your people, and your father's household to the land I will show you . . . and I will bless you. (Genesis 12:1-2)
- I was going! And even though I misunderstood my reasons for going, to this day I still believe God was leading me and knew that I was leaving everything that was important to me in honor of Him. And so did so many of the people I knew in this group. They left their versions of "everything" in a truly heartfelt response to what they believed God wanted them to do. I went. And God did bless!

- I found an amazing place of belonging and of being valued and wanted by the loving members of this church. It was a great place to develop socially in ways I couldn't have even come close to doing in the big, cold world "outside."

- And I eventually met and married the beautiful blond American (not Greek) girl (Becky) I met at college the second day I was there. I am still married to her 45 years later.

- Even though I told her dogmatically that "I'm Greek" and, as a result, we'd probably have three dark-haired sons, three blond daughters later we formed an adorable and greatly blessed little family.

- I eventually became a local elder in the Birmingham church.

- And I had the presumption to aspire for and attain a position that was at the top of our little cultural world. I was hired first as an assistant pastor and then as a full-time pastor between 1989 and 1994 and became the pastor of one of its still-thriving congregations.

I did what I did because I really believed it was what God wanted of me and, surprising as it may seem, God blessed that responsiveness. He did so for me and many others.

Let me show where my heart was, as a Christian, in this cult. I was with God, and God—and yes, even Christ—was with me. He was with the thousands who responded to Him in such simple and sincere and life-changing faith, and in the world of belonging and faith that emanated while we were on that journey.

Again, many would say they've found nothing like it in "mainstream" faith to date. So strange. So thought-provoking. Why?

Chapter 7

THE LOST WORLD OF THE WORLDWIDE

CHURCH OF GOD

W hat was it like in the "cult" in its pre-change heyday? How did the richness of its emphasis on serving God radically and living biblically give it a depth lacking in many doctrinally "correct" churches? Was a cult all poisoned Kool-Aid and compounds? Was it composed of gullible, sheep-like creatures that stupidly succumbed to power-hungry leaders who were simply wolves in sheep's clothing? It is true that you can find story after story of victims in cult history matching these nightmarish narratives, and some I know are from WCG. But I'd be willing to wager you can find those stories in legions of "doctrinally" correct churches as well. In fact, I know you can.

The people I shared life with within this system were some of the most intelligent, sincerest, and God-honoring people I've ever met. They had a passion for God that I've rarely seen. For all the doctrine they had wrong, they had Christ. Or more appropriately, Christ had them. They had him in intellectual and spiritually passionate ways. Many were all-out Spirit-filled Christ-centered Christians.

They were Christians in a cult—but they were still Christians in Christ.

"The" Church in Birmingham

I can still remember the night I went to an outreach event hosted by the local church of the Worldwide Church of God in downtown Birmingham, Alabama. I had to be about seventeen. A bright polished minister delivered an articulate biblically focused address. I don't remember what it was about, but I know I was impressed and not just with what he said. I was impressed with him. He seemed like the kind of guy I would like to be.

I met some of their young people and was impressed by them too. One girl named Lucy had a beauty mark on her face and brown eyes; she reminded me of what I thought a young Marilyn Monroe might look like. She was serving as a greeter. I remember that I gave her a quick sidelong glance to get one more look before I left. In my teenage mind, I hoped the gentle sigh I heard, the raised eyebrows, and the slight smile I saw on her face when she rolled her eyes dreamily as I walked away were hopeful signs that she wanted *me* to come to *her* church. Eventually, I did. But it was not to catch a glimpse of Lucy again; it was to please God (ok, maybe it was both). Somehow, I managed to get my parents to allow me to come to a special Holy Day service. It was to keep the Feast of Weeks, also known as Pentecost, in the late spring of 1972.

Pentecost services are always in late spring. They occur roughly 50 days after the first Sabbath (Saturday) following the annual Passover. It was a special Sabbath, as we called it, so it was a double service. There was one sermon in the morning, and then one in the afternoon after lunch because, after all, special Sabbath day celebrations are mostly about God, or so went the reasoning. Therefore, on a special Sabbath like Pentecost, members gave God a double dose of their attention and got a double dose of God's Word. And sermons "at least" an hour long were part of the program---except when evangelist Gerald Waterhouse spoke. Then you could expect to be there for at least three hours (or until Jesus himself returned and negated the need for a long sermon about his return). And I'm not quite sure that in that culture even Jesus' return would be reason enough to not have to listen to the rest of Mr. Waterhouse's sermon.

A potluck was served in between services. And trust me, people who keep Holy Days and Sabbaths know how to cook. When you can't watch TV and do your home projects, eating is one of the only things you can do other than pray, study, and meditate. So, Sabbath snacks often got very special attention. These folks ate well. Anyway, lo and behold, yet another reward surfaced in my life for serving God by defying my world and going to a Holy Day service. There was Lucy again, at the dessert table, still as pretty as ever and actually remembering me. She said: "Where have you been for so long?" It was definitely a very good moment for me.

Reverential Biblical Focus

But again, I was attracted to more than just this pretty girl who seemed, at least one time, momentarily attracted to me as well. There were people, very sincere and kind people, in attendance. These people seemed to truly believe in the Scripture they were hearing, and reverently took notes as they listened to the sermon. They seemed genuinely interested in hearing what "truth" God wanted them to learn that day. This was not a church concerned with entertaining people so they would come back. These people seemed to have the same "liturgical" passion as people such as my dad had in the Greek Orthodox community. They went to church to serve God and not be served *by* God. They were hungry to serve others as well.

They, like me, had learned there were amazing truths and even power in the Scriptures. These amazing God-breathed words taught you things you never knew about life and God. They could "feed" your soul. They always gave you newer or deeper things to think about and helped you "feel" God. And when you "felt" God, you felt good. You felt joy. You felt light. You felt encouraged. You felt alive.

Every year, every festival, every feast, frequently every Sabbath, it seemed that God taught you something new. And because the audience was willing to be taught, there was consistency in attendance and attention to what was being said. People could and would focus upon and recite "line upon line" and "precept upon precept" (Isaiah 28:10, KJV). You could be like a treasure holder extracting things old and new from those treasures (Matthew 13:52) of truth you derived from that day. When it came to the Scriptures, I'm not sure I've ever discovered a more passionate sense of biblical focus. These people were truly thrilled to discover God's will in the Scripture. They were truly thrilled to understand what God's will was for *them*. When you think about it, that's not being cultish. That's something all Christians should aspire to.

I will forever be grateful to God that I became a pastor in this system. I was paid, in part, to do a lot of study; to be sure, I lived deeply in the Word of God. What a blessing to be able to do just that.

After our doctrinal reformation, it was not uncommon for those in WCG (and later GCI) to bash the heretical ways of the Armstrong era. Perhaps to gain favor with the evangelicals, or perhaps out of embarrassment, they distanced themselves as far as possible. Like me, these folks had mostly grown up in the system, but they often shared narratives completely foreign to my experience. I have sometimes had the same reaction my mother had when she saw the movie *Zorba the Greek*.[18] There's a scene in the film where the village people pillage the home of an eccentric wealthy widow who finally dies. It made them seem almost like looters and scavengers just waiting for her death. My mom sneered dismissively and said, "That's not the Greece I ever lived in."

So, when I hear some of the stories told, or see what seem to be intentional efforts to slime or shame the past with a broad brush, I sometimes feel like saying, "That's not the church I was in."

Now in my resistance to a negative broad brush revisionist narrative, I do not want to fall prey to a broad brush in the opposite way. It was regrettable that WCG's hierarchical ecclesial structure was inherently limiting, and slow to change when change was called for. On one hand, the prejudiced treatment of women and minorities was a reflection of the times, but on the other hand simply a product of poor biblical exegesis. British-Israelism was a crock, and implicitly if not explicitly racist.

Many children raised in this system were pounded with doctrine about laws and rules and "God's prophet Mr. Armstrong" who was never to be questioned. That, plus the often-inexplicable social distancing caused by its eclectic doctrine, deeply hurt them. Our kids went to public schools, but keeping the Sabbath meant no school activities (sports, drama, music) from sundown on Friday to sundown on Saturday.

Meanwhile, the parents, doctrinally challenged but zealous for God and Christ, later suffered the post-trauma of inculcating their kids with what was later admitted to be an unsound worldview. Some families were fractured irreparably as children bucked the doctrine while the parents stayed true. Even my own children suffered from this, not only in the sense of social distancing it created in their lives but in the social void it created when the familiar church structure began to be deconstructed. To them, the framework of their relationship to this world had inexplicably "disappeared." Our doctrinal reformation left them to have to make their way in a world in which both they and their parents had to struggle to reorient.

So, we must avoid the broad brush in both directions. On one hand, I've never seen greater heartfelt expressions of what I consider to be Christianity in my life. On the other hand, we were enmeshed in a problematic doctrinal cult.

In my experience with people in WCG, it wasn't their knowledge and precision of doctrinal interpretation that made them unique. It was their heart. These were a people who truly loved God in a special way. These were a people who really sought to obey the God of the Bible and His Word. I'm here to tell you that God loved them back in experiential ways, and they loved each other in special ways, too. So as a result, no one was insignificant. Everyone was valued and important. They would really stick beside you and have your back, especially if God had called you to be in "the Church."

That's right. It was not called just *a* Church. It was called *the* Church. It was called this because to us that's what it was. It was *the* one true church of God. With gratitude and humility, we saw ourselves as God's honored and special people. And so much of the time, because we believed it to be true, we lived it out!

Another Baptism Rooted in Reality: Something Really Did Happen

Holy Day services were often held in large, rented facilities like an auditorium or armory. I remember attending my first Sabbath services in Birmingham on the second floor of some rented facility downtown. I can remember the diligence of people setting up folding chairs and a stage adorned with flowers and, occasionally, risers for a choir. A bare room was transformed into a God-honoring meeting facility. If you were so moved, you could further honor God and volunteer to set up and takedown.

Sundown at Sabbath meant it was time to visit, to enjoy each other's company, and time to kick back and have fun. Giving God the whole 24-hour period before as "holy" made Saturday nights' peak social events a bit of well-deserved reward and something very special. We'd share many Saturdays after the sun set (thus ending the Sabbath), watching movies, enjoying each other's company in impromptu parties, sharing simple foods, and enjoyable fellowship. An intensity of focus on God the whole day before made for a time of sweet wind down and an intensity of focus on human relationships with whom you had just shared all that focus.

It truly seemed this is what took place when the Bible speaks of the Christian church's first Pentecost:

42 They devoted themselves to the apostles' teaching and to fellowship, to the breaking of bread and to prayer.43 Everyone was filled with awe at the many wonders and signs performed by the apostles.44 All the believers were together and had everything in common.45 They sold property and possessions to give to anyone who had need.46 Every day they continued to meet together in the temple courts. They broke bread in their homes and ate together with glad and sincere hearts,47 praising God and enjoying the favor of all the people. And the Lord added to their number daily those who were being saved. (Acts 2:45-47)

The more and more I got immersed in this kind of spiritual community, the more I got to the point where I decided I wanted to be baptized. Although I'd been baptized as a baby in the Greek Orthodox Church, my new spiritual family didn't believe in the efficacy of infant baptism. And to be honest, I wasn't sure my infant baptism was legitimate. I still wanted more. I chose to be baptized again. I wanted to do so this time because I wanted it to be an intentional choice that I would make for God.

I will admit though, not all my motives were noble. Some of the young people who began attending "the" church about the same time had taken that celebrated next step already. I was feeling left out. If nothing else, I was always competitive. I wanted to be at the top of my class, whatever that class happened to be. Perhaps that was the achieving immigrant child coming out in me. Or, perhaps, that was just a plain carnal desire for preeminence, or at least "co-eminence," with my newly found peers. This go-round in life, "the" church, was my new classroom of achievement. If they were all going to get baptized, well, doggone it, I would too.

I made an appointment with the pastor. He'd become more and more of a hero to me as time passed. Pastors were the local superstars of the system. Their wives were special as well. These women carried great social authority in our world, the way English queens depicted in movies could garner social command in a room by a mere expression. It wasn't done malevolently. These ladies were very sincere in their love for God and sacrificed hours of their husbands' presence as the men served the sometimes very large congregations of God's "one true church."

I shared my request for baptism with my new boyhood hero/coach, the pastor. He smiled at me and was very kind. He seemed a little amused in a good-natured way. I never forgot his words to me. "I see a lot of good understanding in you Jim," he said, "but there's something else I don't see."

What could it be, I wondered?

"It's the fine veneer of repentance."

"The fine veneer of repentance!"

As a teenager, I was bamboozled, to say the least. What did that mean? Looking back, I wonder if he used the word "veneer" wrongly, but it didn't matter. It had the intended effect. I knew he was calling me to something deeper. I knew this man and knew he both lived and stood for way more than a façade of repentance.

Had he been a scheming cult leader, just waiting to weave another unsuspecting victim into his cult web, he could have jumped at the chance to pull another sucker in. But he wasn't like that. Despite the brashness of my youth, this was a sincere man who cared for me and felt he was doing right in God's sight by challenging me.

Undaunted, and too unsophisticated to be embarrassed or insulted, I made a follow-up appointment. If he wanted to see repentance, he was going to see it. In what I'm sure should have been at least an Oscar-nominated performance, I poured it on thick. I probably was up there with the most affecting of the televangelists who have repented publicly on television. It was more performance than repentance. Ironically, I chuckle to think I was pouring on more layers of veneer!

I was partly surprised when he agreed to baptize me. He may have seen right through me, but in the end, perhaps he saw my eagerness. Maybe he was remembering that God's kindness leads us to repentance, and decided just to entrust my situation to God.

He was right to do so. Because God did act.

Weeks went by. I heard nothing about a date being set for my baptism. I assumed maybe my performance had failed, and I'd be trying again at some point in the future. In the meantime, I still was growing in grace and knowledge, and developing a personal relationship with God. While I was probably competitive in this baptismal quest, I was very sincere about my relationship with God. I prayed often and sincerely. I remember one Sabbath morning praying in an unusually focused way before church, in an inspired way that surprised even me.

Somewhere in that prayer, I came to this overwhelming conviction: I truly needed to give myself to God. I wasn't even thinking about my baptism. I was praying, I believe, inspired by God's Spirit. I remember suddenly being led to say certain words. I paused a bit before I said them because I knew if I said them, I had to mean them.

I said: "God, whatever you want me to do, that's what I'm going to do."

Then after letting the gravity of that statement sink in, I repeated it, listening to my own words: "Whatever you want me to do, that's what I'm going to do."

It was as if someone else was speaking through me and with me, as if I was being lost in the words, baptized in them, or better yet baptized in the Word Himself, before being baptized by water! Looking back, I was participating in the greater reality that is best expressed by Scripture and by which all religious observances are contextualized:

> *Therefore do not let anyone judge you by what you eat or drink, or with regard to a religious festival, a New Moon celebration, or a Sabbath day. These are a shadow of the things that were to come; the reality, however, is found in Christ.* (Colossians 2:17)

Without meaning to, I had found godly repentance or what the Bible calls *metanoia*, a radical change of mind. Instead of attaining reality with my performance as if I were up against the wall, I was beginning to understand that Reality had found me and given me a spacious place of freedom in which to change:

> *"He brought me out into a spacious place; he rescued me because he delighted in me."*
> (Psalm 18:19)

I ended my prayer, got dressed, and was picked up by my ride to afternoon Sabbath services. I mingled with the crowd and was confused when someone came up to me and said:

"Congratulations!"

"For what?" I responded.

"For what's happening today," he said. "You're getting baptized."

Apparently, they had put me on the list. My repentance performance with the pastor *had* succeeded. But God saw to it that it was more than just a performance. He granted me true repentance in that prayer in a way only He could, and right after it, I was to be baptized. It came together in a way too orchestrated to be just a coincidence. Christ was with me, even though I was in a cult.

I remember hastily borrowing a change of clothes from a buddy who had an apartment nearby.

I was baptized into the body of Jesus Christ, and hands were laid on me that I might receive the Holy Spirit. I felt no wind, heard no bells, and sensed no whistles. There were no lightning strikes. Nothing overtly charismatic happened. But as I was being driven home, I sensed something that I had never sensed before. I was aware of something, a calmness, a feeling of peace and security, a peaceful Presence inside me that I had never experienced before. It was a calm and calming Presence that gave me a smile of assurance. I believe with all my heart and soul the Holy Spirit moved in me in a deeper and more palpable way.

The Scripture says:

Draw nigh to Him and He will draw nigh to you. (James 4:8, KJV)

Retrospectively considering my baptism, I was participating in Christ in his relationship with the Father, and in the power of the Spirit I sensed God's nearness to me and His love for me as his beloved son. Despite any twisted doctrine, I was a Spirit-filled Christian.

I was a Christian—a real Christian—in a real cult. And Christ was within me, and working within me and my context, every step of the way.

Chapter 8

SITTING AT THE TOP

OF WORLDWIDE'S WORLD

The week after my baptism, I remember making my regular financial donation that I would mail to denominational headquarters, but this time I attached an extra note. It was inspired by, of all people, a song sung by one of my favorite singers (and, I believe, a bit of an armchair theologian as well). The song was "People,"[19] by Barbra Streisand.

Still filled with a continuous and stable sense of the Spirit's new, more constant Presence, I so resonated with these words that I included them in this note to whoever would be processing that donation.

A feeling deep in my soul, says I was half, now I'm whole.

"I got baptized," I added.

"Thank you."

Yes, I was in a cult. Yes, I had left a rich Technicolor orthodox church for a non-orthodox one. But fellowship with these fiercely biblical, humble people gave me something I hadn't experienced in my Greek expression of faith. Maybe it was a matter of timing. My Greek Orthodox childhood was a God-soaked environment, but it didn't sink in the same way. Now I had a deeper sense of God. It is one that has never gone away.

I believe He led me to my next steps. I applied to and was accepted into Ambassador College in Big Sandy, Texas. It was one of the denomination's three Bible schools. It was also a "finishing" school of sorts for aspiring young people who wanted to engage more deeply in our system. Young people who went there were often the ones who showed the most promise in the local church communities. And young people who were accepted were truly given the best the organization had to offer. Granted, this was enabled by members who loyally paid up to three tithes a year to God's "one true church," and I don't mean to justify or excuse that. But many contributed to it, recognizing it was in effect a fishing pool, and a finishing school, for the organization's future leaders.

It was a status symbol to say you'd been accepted to Ambassador College. I had the grades; I had the recommendations; I had the hunger to go to what I considered one of God's three true colleges on the face of the Earth. They were all beautifully landscaped, with well-appointed facilities that were well-maintained and well-staffed. We had intelligent, articulate faculty who theologically and philosophically could take our understanding to the next level. We were even granted respected academic accreditation. We were given travel experiences, performance experiences, and social experiences.

At Ambassador I developed socially in ways I had never seemed able to do in my previous life setting. A lot of this had to do with the fact that the second day I was there I met the young lady who would become my wife.

Becky was a beauty, to be sure. But it was more than just her physical beauty that attracted me. It was her inner fire, her inner tenacity. I was attracted to the fact that Becky sought to obey God with all her heart, even when her family, who weren't on the same page at all, kicked her out of their home when she felt she needed to keep the Sabbath no matter what. Becky had the courage to face this brave new world of giving it all up for God alone, with just God. That's what brought her to Ambassador College, and thankfully into my path.

In the environment of this fascinating, accepting, and often very kind and concerned world created at this college, even a diamond in the very rough like me began to receive some badly needed cutting and polishing. I went from being the awkward kid who had a hard time finding a place in normal society, to an accepted one who had a place in this world. When you're in a "little pond," when you're in God's one true church, when you're one of God's specially called young people, guess what? You're special! You begin to believe you are special. You're worth going the extra mile for, to train and ready for the future, even if you are a bit of a sow's ear.

Seeking the Path of Ministry

I graduated. I was never anyone's top pick for becoming a pastor. And I wasn't one of the flashy, showy, popular people either. I managed to evade and eventually drop out of public speaking courses. In fact, I hated public speaking and was horrible at it.

No one saw in me God's sign saying, "Future Pastor in the Making." That included my wife-to-be. There was one young man she did have sort of a crush on. It was one of the pastoral hopefuls, but not just a hopeful, mind you. This was someone who had been pegged as destined to become a pastor. Becky stopped dating him intentionally. She had decided that the last thing she wanted to be was a pastor's wife. She wanted to align herself with someone who most certainly would never be a pastor. She chose to date and, eventually, marry me. I wasn't on anyone's future pastor list.

As Becky and I fell in love, I learned in wonder how God enabled her to win back her parent's hearts and witness the love of God to them. She had the ability to put things in amazing perspective with words of wisdom. And she had the ability to stand up to me when I needed to be stood up to. In fact, she had the ability to stand up to anybody when they needed to be stood up to! And for forty years again and again she has stood up *with* me and *for* me for the sake of truth and the gospel.

I'll never forget when I took Becky "home to meet Mama." Mama served my tiny fiancé a giant plate of spaghetti with burnt butter Greek-style, multiple portions of meat, a huge salad with Feta cheese and Kalamata olives, and slices of French bread made by a Greek. As she was sitting behind this piled-high plate, Daddy finally asked her, "Do you want something to drink?" Overwhelmed and at a loss of what else to say, she said meekly, "Milk." And then my father produced a glass that had to hold at least half a quart of whole (not fat-reduced) milk. I could barely see my fiancé for the food.

After graduation, I went back home to Birmingham. My father helped me get a job at the power company where he worked and where I would work for the next twelve years. It was a season full of family love. Amazing Becky gave birth to our three amazing daughters. We made lasting friendships in our local WCG church and saw parts of the world through our "festivals" (more on that later) that we might never have seen otherwise.

But something was still missing. I still desperately wanted to teach God's Word. I wanted to feed people with what God fed me—His wonderful Word! Miraculously, He enabled me to do so. I started out by speaking little mini messages before sermons called sermonettes. In our world, it was an honor to be chosen to do so. But even a sermonette for me was quite the intimidating experience. I remember not wearing my glasses or contacts so I couldn't see the people's faces. I would walk up to the podium, hold it tight, and open my mouth. God just began speaking through me. Eloquently. Interestingly. Intelligently. At least that's what people said. And I knew this wasn't just me. Left to my own devices, I was terrible at it. But once again, I had prayed, and God coupled my desire to teach God's Word with a gift to me of communicating it.

I continued to grow and was hired to be a ministerial trainee in my hometown. I got cold feet and bowed out. Then I sank into a depression about what I'd given up, and graciously God gave me a second chance. I was hired to be a pastoral trainee in Raleigh, North Carolina. I would help pastor a two-church circuit of God's "one true church" in the Raleigh-Rocky Mount area. I made many beloved friends and enjoyed the denomination in its heyday. The church was stable and well respected. The people were loving and kind. My kids found places of belonging in the denomination's well-developed youth program that successfully provided alternative activities for youth who missed out on Friday night activities and Saturday sports because of the Sabbath. Unlike the outside world, everybody belonged. The most awkward boy could get a spot on the basketball team. The quietest girl could become a cheerleader. It was an amazing world within a world that many young people truly missed after our doctrinal changes came and they were plunged into a colder, less embracing culture outside.

A Recollection of an Old Worldview October 1989

It is the fall, and my family and I are excited, anxious, and happy as we prepare for our annual trip to the place where God has placed His name. Becky and I and our three young daughters have carefully saved our festival tithe, ten percent of our entire income, to rejoice as the Lord our God has commanded through His servant Moses in His Word in Deuteronomy 14. This is our second tithe, which is to be used only "in the presence of the Lord… at the place he will choose as a dwelling for his name":

Be sure to set aside a tenth of all that your fields produce each year. Eat the tithe of your grain, new wine and olive oil, and the firstborn of your herds and flocks in the presence of the LORD your God at the place he will choose as a dwelling for his Name, so that you may learn to revere the LORD your God always (Deuteronomy 14:22-23).

It is not to be confused with our first tithe, which is to be given regularly to God's servants, or our third tithe, which is saved at the end of every three years for the Levites (our ministry workers and pastors), the fatherless and widows (Deuteronomy 14: 29).* This annual tithe of all our increase is to be spent in one eight-day period at the Festival of Tabernacles. We can buy whatever we like to eat (as long as it's not unclean, of course): "...cattle, sheep, wine or other fermented drink. . . anything you wish" it says (Deuteronomy 14:26)! Imagine, living off one-tenth of your income for an entire year in one compressed eight-day period! What a positive picture that paints of the extravagant blessings associated with a world totally under the reign of Christ's Kingdom of God. It's a taste of the promised land "flowing with milk and honey" (Exodus 3:8).

We are so looking forward to living in temporary dwellings (for us nice hotels), eating the best of the land (at the best restaurants) with happy festivalgoers, meeting new friends from all over the land, and bonding with them over many a fine meal and worship service. At these services, we will once again learn the glories of the coming (not yet here) Kingdom of God—because that is, after all, what these days represent.

Yes, we must use this tithe properly—for food, strong drink, and lodging, just as Moses gave instructions for all of God's people for all time. We must make sure that we rejoice because as Nehemiah told us: "The joy of the Lord is your strength" (Nehemiah 8:10). But we must be careful not to be selfish too. We must remember the widow, the fatherless, and the Levites, our ministers of the Lord, who serve us, teach us and often own no property because of their unique calling and lifestyle in God's way.

By now you've gathered that I am not an Old Testament Israelite in the glory days of Hezekiah's celebrations. At this point in time, I'm a white-collar professional living

---

* See Deuteronomy 14:28-29 and Deuteronomy 26:12 about this tithe. It was to be sent in every three years (counted from the date of your baptism) and used to fund those we considered "Levites" (pastors) and to give financial assistance to widows and those in need. So every third year you were paying your taxes, three tithes and living off of half of your normal income. And there are people who would line up and tell you stories about how they seemed to prosper materially that year more than other "two-tithe" only years (the "first" tithe that went to Headquarters, and the "second" tithe collected yearly to fund your Festival and Holy Day observances). Imagine what it was like living off of a tenth of your total income for an 8-day Festival period, and you'll perhaps get a "feel" for why these Festivals became such fond memories for many.

in Birmingham, Alabama. It is the late 1980s. I am traveling to our appointed festival site in St. Petersburg, Florida. We've been all over the country to other sites in other years: Pasadena, California; Norfolk, Virginia; Lake of the Ozarks, Missouri. One year we even went to the Camber Sands Resort in southern England, not too far from the White Cliffs of Dover. No, I'm not an ancient Israelite. I'm a Greek-American Christian in the Worldwide Church of God. I'm driving a 1986 Nissan Sentra loaded with a wife, three daughters, and a recently purchased (and hastily assembled) car top carrier, preparing to spend some $3,500 in one week as a symbol of the "World Tomorrow" at a Festival of Tabernacles celebration sponsored by my church. I will be joining some 7,000 other brethren of the "one true church" (as I saw it then) that by God's grace had somehow managed to preserve the key to biblical understanding—the true set of biblical days meant to be observed by Christians. We had the "true" days that would reveal—if only people would keep them—the true picture of salvation history.

As we travel to the location where the Lord has placed his name, our journey takes us into the night. Becky is busy settling down the excited children (after all, we had taken them out of school for the week). Overhead hangs what, in some circles, is called the Hunter's Moon. We smile at this because we know that, in fact, it is the Festival Moon, which always comes after the Day of Atonement, and always precedes the first night of the Festival. How in sync it seems that even nature responds to the true Festival cycle of the Lord our God! But of course, it would, because God gave these things to be signs in the heavens, days and seasons, months and years, as it said in Genesis 1:14.

The heathen, those of the nations around us, including those of the "paganized" Christianity that dominates our nation, try to worship God in the dead of winter with a celebration of Christ's birth (never biblically commanded anywhere, mind you!) nowhere near the time it probably actually occurred. In the spring they seem to parallel the true biblical worship days of Leviticus 23 with so-called "resurrection" (Easter) services. These services are replete with symbols of rabbits and chickens and eggs and other fertility symbols that surely must be an affront to our God. God told us plainly in Deuteronomy 12:29-32 that we were not to worship the LORD our God like the nations did their gods. He warned us through the prophet Daniel that the people of God must be careful, because one would come and deceive God's people from His true ways, "and try to change the set times and the laws" (Daniel 7:25)—times and laws about sacred worship times, of course. That is exactly what most conventional Christianity, Christianity "falsely so-called," had done. That's exactly what the "great whore" of Revelation 17—the Catholic Church—-had done, and her weak-willed "harlot" daughters, the Protestant churches, had followed suit. As a result, they had lost sight of God's true master plan of salvation, putting such unnecessary focus on the work of the person of Jesus Christ at his first coming! But that wasn't going to happen to us, because we had found the key to true biblical understanding, the keeping of the true biblical days, the only days truly commanded in the Bible. And they alone depicted the true picture of salvation history or, as we called it, the Master Plan of Salvation.

Following the list given in Leviticus 23, I muse over what days I kept and what those days taught me. First, the Passover, kept on the evening of Nisan 14th, the Hebrew month in the spring corresponding roughly to our March or April. This festival pictured the true way the Christ was to be celebrated by picturing the true escape from slavery to sin that Satan made possible by the death of the Passover lamb, Jesus Christ. You really had to be sincere about this service; you couldn't take it inappropriately per instruction in 1 Corinthians 11. I remember spending days before the service reading about Jesus' journey to Jerusalem, putting myself in his shoes, trying to figure out what he was thinking, feeling, wanting as he faced the horrors of the cross and gave his all to God. I bonded with him in that process. I know I did. Christ my Passover was sacrificed for me! Therefore, let us keep the Feast (1 Corinthians 5:7-8). And that's exactly what we did.

The week-long Days of Unleavened Bread Festival, which immediately followed, taught us that even though Christ died for our sins, we must work hard to do our part, to put the leaven of sin out of our lives. Just as we removed leavened bread and leavening products from our homes for a perfect seven-day period in the spring, we reminded ourselves that we must strive to live lives of growing in holy, righteous character by continuing to put sin out of our lives and working actively to do so. By growing enough in holy, righteous character, we would hopefully qualify to stand before Christ at his coming. And be warned—if we didn't work sufficiently, we might not overcome and qualify to be saved!

The Protestant and Catholic churches not only failed to keep the true days of the Bible, but they also set aside only one day, not even a special Sabbath, to focus on Christ's work on the Cross (Good Friday). Meanwhile, as was commanded for the observation of Unleavened Bread, we in the one true church dedicated a whole seven-day period, with two commanded convocations and two Sabbaths and a lot of work cleaning "leaven" and leavened foods (including bread, cookie, and cracker crumbs that had accumulated during the year) out from our homes, our cars, our offices, or our anything *else!** It was obvious that God wanted the greater emphasis to be put on what you must do to strive to stay saved after you're saved.*

Next came the Feast of Weeks (Pentecost), kept fifty days after the first Sunday of the Days of Unleavened Bread, commemorating the first, small harvest of souls that would be won to the Kingdom of God in this age. It was fitting that this feast came in the spring of the year when only the smaller, barley harvest was reaped in ancient Israel. That taught us that the harvest of true Christianity was really much smaller than the world realized, because so few of the world's Christians accepted the true Sabbaths and Holy Days, the only true signs of who the few true Christians were in this world.

There was a pause in the summer of observances, and then the fall festivals would kick in when most of God's true work of salvation was going to be done. First would come the Festival of Trumpets on the first day of the seventh month, Tishri, falling roughly in a September/October time frame, depicting the pivotal event of all salvation history, even greater than the death of Christ on the cross—the second coming of Jesus Christ. He would come at the "voice of the archangel" and "the trumpet call of God" (1 Thessalonians 4:13-17), hence the association of Christ's second coming with trumpets and thus the mystery of the "Day of Trumpets" revealed. The dead would rise and would be transformed and be with the Lord forever.

Since the Messiah's feet were going to "stand on the Mount of Olives" on that day (Zechariah 14:4), it was obvious that we were going to be with the Lord on the Earth (since that's where his feet landed when he returned). We would reign with him as kings and priests "on the earth" (and not in heaven, as Christians "falsely so-called" were taught). You could read that in Revelation 5:10 in the King James Version of the Bible. This was the central festival of the seven-festival plan in Leviticus 23, surely

---

* Just to share how I truly believe God was with us as we engaged in this process, even in humorous ways, I'll share this story. In true obedient zeal, I had pulled out the back seat of our little Renault Alliance to truly clean an area I was sure was filled with bread, cookie, and cracker crumbs consumed by our three little daughters throughout our many journeys to church and Festivals in our car. And true enough, it was laden with all of the above, and in my thought, world needed to be cleaned out. But I also feel God had a special joke in store just for me that day. It was both a sign of His sense of humor and His love. Just as I pulled out the back car seat, there was something I didn't expect to see in the middle of what was a truly "leavened" crumb nightmare. It was an upturned Scripture card I'd been using to memorize the Scriptures, and it apparently had made its way underneath our back seat. It had a very special message for me that year. It was 1 Corinthians 2:9. It pronounced, in solemn King James language, a truth I was living out in that very exhausting moment of thorough cleaning: 9 But as it is written, Eye hath not seen, nor ear heard, neither have entered into the heart of man, the things which God hath prepared for them that love him (1 Corinthians 2:9 KJV). That is, until you zealously pull out the backseat to properly get all the leaven so you can keep the Days of Unleavened Bread in the Worldwide Church of God.

proving that it was his second coming in world-ruling power and glory, not his lowly first coming that was meant to be the crux of all history.

Then the Day of Atonement would come with its mysterious two-goat ritual. And Aaron shall cast lots upon the two goats; one lot for the LORD, and the other lot for the scapegoat. (Leviticus 16:8) That true day opened for us a major understanding "missed" by Christians who were keeping the days Satan had slyly insinuated into the early church. You see, it wasn't true that both goats represented Christ—only the "one for the LORD" did. The other one, the one allowed to live, the Azazel goat, represented the evil one, Satan, which was banished to the wilderness just as Satan would be banished to the Abyss after Christ's return in Revelation 20. True justice would be served only when Satan's role was properly emphasized, and he received his just due. How brilliant of God to help us focus on the work of Satan with this day, rather than deceiving us with a diluted focus on the work and person of Jesus Christ in his first coming, like the deceived Christian world did.

Once Satan was banished, and judgment was rightly placed on his head, that positioned us for the next great event of God's master plan, the 1000-year Millennium, where Christ and the saints would reign over the Earth and the true, great "harvest" of souls would be won to God. After all, since Satan had been banished, his deceptive work would no longer stand in the way. There would then be a great harvest of souls.

And wouldn't you know it! The very next festival in God's Master Plan of Salvation was the Feast of Tabernacles, the Feast of Booths, the great harvest festival, picturing the great harvest of souls destined to come only after the Second Coming of Jesus Christ. What the Festival of Tabernacles taught us was that riches, wealth, overflowing physical abundance—what those of ancient Israel experienced when they celebrated their agricultural harvest—was the true destiny of all true Sabbath-keeping Christians. This apex harvest festival represented the overflowing end-time "harvest of souls" (like our end-season harvest of crops) to the Lord that would take place only after the true pivotal event of history, which was not just the first coming of Christ, or his death on the Cross, as was mistakenly assumed by many.

Christ's death on the cross was very important; so important that it was the first of the biblical observances. But the true pivotal event of history was the Second Coming of Christ when he would return in world-ruling power and glory to the sound of trumpets, as the Feast of Trumpets showed! It's the Second Coming of Christ that would have the ultimate impact. The culmination was the Last Great Day of the Feast (Leviticus 23:39; John 7:37), which pictured the Great White Throne Judgment period, as we called it (Revelation 20:11-15), when all the unsaved dead would rise and be given their true and final chance to accept salvation and the true knowledge of God's true days.

To think that we'd know nothing of all this—until we discovered the center of our doctrinal understanding—the seventh-day Sabbath. What an incredible way to look at the world. What an incredible way to relate to it. What an incredible worldwide association it put me in. What deep biblical engagement it gave me. What an incredible "world within a world" it created. We had worship services and festivals all over the world. We had networks of friends and members that had bonded over many a fine worship service and many a fine meal during festival times. We had bonded closely in the national church youth association created to give our children athletic and social opportunities in a world in which many of their "normal" opportunities for such things fell on God's true rest days. Deep bonding took place as we defied norms, lost jobs because we wouldn't work on the Sabbath, and alienated families by refusing to participate in their unfortunate "pagan" annual gatherings like Christmas and Easter. But we developed many fine new relationships with others who knew the truth about the days and worked hard to obey them. We were God's true church. A special people. Yes, indeed, a peculiar treasure.

It was a joy to ride together, and to think of these things, as we headed to the Feast. We had a unique place in the world, and a unique worldwide family to whom we belonged. We had a way of looking at the world that made sense to us. We had the true picture of salvation history and the true days that went with them. We had the right rituals, and because of that, we and we alone had the right version of the story.

That was the forever-lost world of the congregations of the Worldwide Church of God. It's a world many to this day regret no longer having. In a way, I do too---not that I miss the wrong doctrinal understanding. But I miss being in a place where people hung on every word of the Bible for just one more "new" truth, where they'd truly and experientially with sincere hearts took stands for God. And where you found a people who really did love you the way you'd think people who loved the Bible would. For all that we misunderstood orthodox doctrine, God understood *us*. And there are so many who would say He was with us then in intense and special ways.

It was a world that was undeniably spiritual, and yet as I look back on it, so deeply troubling.

Chapter 9

THE DOCTRINAL SHOT HEARD 'ROUND THE
WHOLE "WORLDWIDE" WORLD

I found myself in a strange place in the period between 1993 and 1994. There were rumors that something called "the changes" was about to be released. There was a sense that whatever was coming down the pike was going to be life-changing. I remember at the time I was reading a book called *The Egyptian*, by Finnish author Mika Waltari.[20] It spoke of Pharaoh Akhenaten's failed attempt to do away with the ancient Egyptian gods and bring Egypt into the worship of the "one true god," the Sun God. The old priests simmered with discontent until, finally, they were able to overthrow this new system and bring people back into mainstream Egyptian belief of a pantheon of gods.

I saw from that story what happened in a culture where change for some "greater truth" was more than the culture could bear. I remember having a vague sense that something similar was about to happen in our lives. I simply had a premonition that some kind of epic religious change was going to overturn our world, and that like in the novel I had just read, there would be power struggles to keep the old system in power. In a way, what we went through was going to reflect much of what I had read.

Here's the behind-the-scenes story.

A New Administration is Given Charge of the Denomination

After the elder Armstrong died in January 1986, he was succeeded by Joseph W. Tkach, Sr. A former union leader and later a superintendent of ministers, Tkach saw himself as more of an administrator than a charismatic personality as Armstrong had been. Capable in his own right, Tkach did not hesitate to assign other people besides himself to speak nationally for the organization and he was not too threatened to seek the expertise of others for doctrinal questions.

A primal element of our salvation story did indeed include a commitment to ongoing biblical study and a willingness to change when proven wrong. No longer under the shadow of Armstrong's dominating personality, Tkach repeatedly saw places where he came to feel we were doctrinally unsound. At first, he made minor doctrinal changes in areas about the benefit of medical help, celebrating birthdays, and the use of cosmetics for women. As time ensued, he also realized that other things Armstrong had emphasized couldn't be proven scripturally, so he began to downplay even the prophetic speculations that had made the television program and *Plain Truth* magazine so interesting. Questions arose about more and more of the things that Armstrong had written, and some of his books were withdrawn from circulation until further study could resolve the questions. Even though some members were concerned, most remained loyal to the organization.

Many of the issues that came under review had to do with the heavy emphasis given to the return of Christ as being central to the salvation story. And so it was that the Worldwide Church of God eventually came to see how the biblical focus of the salvation story—what Paul said was "of first importance" in 1 Corinthians 15—was the death and resurrection of Jesus Christ. It also came to see that it misunderstood what it meant to be "born again." It began to pull away from the long-standing teaching of British-Israelism, which again basically asserted that the descendants of all Anglo-Saxons were descendants of the lost tribes of Israel (and hence should be Sabbath-keepers). It began to understand the divinity and personhood of the Holy Spirit and accepted a more mainstream doctrine of the Trinity.

Finally came the most traumatic change of all. This little, but tightly knit and, at that time financially and administratively sound, fellowship began to learn that it was truly under the New—not the Old—Covenant. In his message announcing this change, Tkach would explain that Christians do not have to keep Old Covenant laws such as the weekly and annual Sabbaths. "In many ways, the Sabbath had been the foundational doctrine of the entire denomination," a church history reported . . . "this was the biggest change of all."21*

For the vast majority in the fellowship, both minister and lay member alike, this biggest change of all was made public by Tkach in a sermon message that was delivered via videotape on Saturday, December 24, 1994. As an associate pastor of the Wilson, North Carolina congregation, I sat with eyes glued to the television screen, along with 120 other members in the auditorium of Wilson High School, where our local congregation of the church had recently moved. The rumor mill had been rumbling for several weeks. As one member of our local church had observed, we were about to hear "the shot that was going to be heard around the world."

During three short hours, Tkach, reading from a 62-page single-spaced sermon script, indeed did more than just fire a single shot. To many, he dropped a bombshell of information, exploding and shattering concepts that had formulated a lifetime's worth of worldviews. Speaking to thousands of us who had estranged families, lost jobs, and based whole careers around the concept that conventional Christian worship was devilishly pagan, and that only "biblical" days must be kept—he began to tell us the following "new" truths (as we would have put it):

- The church is no longer under the Old Covenant but, in fact, is a New Covenant organism.
- Salvation is by faith through grace and is not gained in the least through law-keeping.
- Members who needed to work on Saturday were not committing sin.22

And as if that was not enough, we were later going to learn that the other Festival Sabbath days listed in Leviticus 23 were no longer necessary. They were not necessary to truly see "the whole plan of God" as we had taught and believed. Indeed, you could see "the whole plan of God" in the simple story of the life, death, and resurrection of Jesus Christ!

This was being told to a group of people who had seen a church built around these very same joint meeting times and celebrations. We had bonded in a complex network of associations based on years of spending Sabbaths,

---

* The history given in the preceding paragraphs and the ones following rely heavily on the work from which this quote was taken as well.

festivals, and other activities together. It was indeed "a shot" —and a shock— both heard and felt around the whole of "Worldwide's" world.

It has been a fascinating study to witness the after-effects of that shock. Immediately after the changes, some 12,000 members left and formed one of many splinter groups that have sprung from our fellowship. Thousands more stopped attending any church, and many congregations were left with only half the members they used to have. Church income dropped fifty percent, and hundreds of employees were laid off.

With pastors leaving in droves, I found myself pastoring four churches at one time (two in Indiana and two in Ohio), as well as attempting to learn all I could through the now-approved process of seminary training and consulting with fellow Christians from other groups. Friends and families were split. It was a time of anguish and depression and some hard realizations. We'd gotten the "story" wrong because our emphasis was never on the story of Christ but on our own stories and, in this case, some ritual day observances that were integral to our stories.

We had been Christians, but Christians in a very cultic expression of the faith. Christ was with us and blessed us, but our energies had been diverted into keeping days and building a world around that context. We were not as effective in sharing the true Gospel as we could have been, because our focus was on being Christians in a cult, more than on being Christians in Christ.

That was all about to change. And the change was very difficult indeed.

The Loss of My Whole World View

My worldview was turned totally upside down by Tkach's presentation on that December 24, 1994. Reflective of the denomination at large, half of our local people left our church almost immediately. But many of us hung in together and began to process this new "plain truth." Many of my fellow congregations and I began to see salvation history differently.

Looking back, there's one part of the story that has not changed. I may have been laboring under, limited by, and imprisoned in wrong doctrine—but I was a Christian. Christ was with me. So, I seriously had this question: "Lord, if it's not about the Sabbath, what is it about now?"

Chapter 10

TRYING TO TAKE THE

"CULT" OUT OF AN EX-CULT

I could elaborate further on the theological changes I made as I accepted what had been for a while 'the unbelievable," but here's the long and short of it.

We had been very right in one sense. Yet in another sense, we had been very wrong! We had been right in believing in the holiness of the Bible. We were right in believing that it was the ultimate source for our doctrine and understanding. We were right in believing in an "all-out" response to God and what He wanted of us as taught in His written Word. We had been right in believing that Jesus meant it when He said to love the Lord your God with all your heart and all your mind and all your soul and all your strength. We were right in believing you should live by every word that comes out of the mouth of God.

We had been right in committing ourselves to the study and restudy of Scripture, always willing to learn new and deeper truth. We had been right in being willing to give up everything and anything for God and living a life of passionate Word-directed responsiveness. We had been right in our sense of God's love for us and our dedication and our loyalty to loving each other in fellowship.

But we had been wrong in our "rightly dividing the Word of truth" (1 Timothy 2:15, KJV). Hence, we were wrong in understanding what God wanted of us. It wasn't the keeping of the Sabbath and Holy Days as if these "elemental"* observances had efficacy and power in and of themselves. No! There was a greater reality, we learned.

> *These are a shadow of the things that were to come; the reality, however, is found in Christ.* (Colossians 2:17)

This was the reality that I had experienced at times despite all the wrong doctrine!

The "reality," *the* Truth was not a *what*. The Truth was a *Who*. Jesus said plainly:

> *"I am the Way, **the Truth**, and the Life."* (John 14:6, emphasis mine)

When you really understand this, it changes everything. It even changes your approach to something as sacred as the Ten Commandments, which was our basis for understanding the need to keep the Sabbath.

A New Approach to the Ten Commandments

The fact that the Sabbath was indeed one of the Ten Commandments made it a no-brainer to many of us for years that it should be kept, but in our doctrinal reformation, we learned something that many Christians and Jews have yet to recognize. Indeed, it was the Jew-turned Apostle, Paul of Tarsus, who from first-hand experience taught that a relationship with Jesus was deeper than any religious observance. Even the Ten Commandments, Paul states, have been so misused as to be part of the ministry that brought death, not life.

Did you hear that? The Ten Commandments, the ministry engraved on tablets of stone, was part of a ministry that brought death! Read it yourself:

> *Now if the ministry that brought death, which was engraved in letters on stone, came with glory, so that the Israelites could not look steadily at the face of Moses*

---

* In Galatians 4:2, Paul speaks of being subjected to "elemental spiritual forces" in a phase of spiritual immaturity. Probably misunderstanding the real meaning of the verse, I began to feel that in Christ, I was being led to graduate from serving God by focusing on something as "elemental" as a 24-hour period (the Sabbath day). Later in this chapter, Paul speaks of people who were "slaves to those who by nature were not gods" (verse 8), being under the same "weak and miserable" (verse 9) "forces." This was a reference back to those same "elemental" spiritual forces discussed in verse 2. I perhaps did not understand all the nuances conveyed by the word. But I did come to rightly believe that my response to God had indeed been a very "elemental" one. It was time to spiritually begin to grow up and move toward Christ.

because of its glory, transitory though it was, will not the ministry of the Spirit be even more glorious? (2 Corinthians 3:7-8)

It's not that the Ten Commandments, or any of the laws of God, were evil or wrong. It's not that the individual commands given should not in almost every case be lived out literally, as appropriate considering the revelation of God's Son, Jesus Christ. The truth of the matter is that obedience to God's will in the Ten Commandments is found in obedience to Christ by the Holy Spirit, and apart from Christ the commandments are too easily co-opted by the flesh, working *against* grace instead of participating *in* grace. And it follows that because anything that is of the flesh is of death, to the extent the Ten Commandments are co-opted into a fleshly works-oriented system, they are of death too. Astoundingly, the written code itself became "the ministry that brought death, which was engraved in letters on stone" (2 Corinthians 3:7). This reorientation was a bitter pill for some of us in WCG, and it was vivifying for others.

We were like those whom the Apostle Paul reproached for a spiritually "dull-hearted" reading of the Old Covenant, at the heart of which was the Ten Commandments (2 Corinthians 3:14 ff). The glory was never from the Ten Commandments themselves (Moses had actually put a veil over his face to keep the Israelites from seeing the mountaintop glory gradually fade away). The glory was from Jesus Christ, the rock struck by Moses from whom living water flowed (1 Corinthians 10:4). But because we had the cart before the horse when it came to the true source of glory, our minds had been "dulled" when we read the Old Covenant. Only in Christ was the veil that covered our hearts taken away. Salvation was not affected by what day we kept but by what Lord we focused on. Intuitively we knew this because we'd been in Him all along! We saw through the brokenness of religion and religious leaders and a system based on law rather than on an eternal reality we share intuitively with Christ and as revealed in the glory of the Holy Spirit:

> *"Now the Lord is the Spirit, and where the Spirit of the Lord is, there is freedom."*
> (2 Corinthians 3:17)

We were free! It was mind-boggling, but it was true. And that changed everything. The things I thought I had to do to follow God radically I no longer had to do!

"So now what?" I asked.

"Go Take Care of Your People"

Believe it or not, there was no bitterness in me at that time for having left my family and my beloved Greek culture for those many years. I knew God had led me. I knew that my lack of "knowing the way of God more adequately" (Acts 18:26) did not keep me from being a Christian. I knew that God loved me and was with me even while doctrinally I was in a cult.

What I had done, I'd done for God. What so many of my peers had done, they had done for God. I knew that. And bless his heart, so did my Orthodox dad. When he and my mom heard about the changes, Mama, the Greek village girl, said in her wonderful street-smart way (try to read this with an accent and be sure to trill the letter "r"): "Jimmy, now you can be G-rrr-eek prrr-iest and have a condo in Flo-rri-da and make $75,000 a year." (This was in 1994. I guess that's what their priest made. I imagine he's gotten a few cost of living raises since then. I remember making $26,900 as a WCG pastor for several years).

Daddy was a little bit more spiritually profound in his reaction. "Jimmy," he said, with tears in his eyes, knowing what an immense turn of life focus this must have been for me, "You go home now and take care of your people."

I want you to consider how truly sacrificial, how truly spiritually profound this was. He knew I could have come back to his beloved Greek Orthodox Church. He knew I could fulfill his own dreams and maybe let him see one of his own sons enter Orthodox ministry. He would have loved that if I did. But he also knew that Christianity wasn't always about doing what was best for *you*.

Just because our doctrine was wrong, didn't mean all the widows, old ladies, loyal members, and their children, those still looking for fellowship, still looking for direction, weren't our responsibility, weren't our people to take care of. If there was a time any of these ever needed stability, or some form of it, now was it.

So, I did what Dad told me to do. I went home to care for "my people"— God's people in the Worldwide Church of God—whom God still loved. If anybody needed reassurance at this time, they did. They needed someone to help them not throw out the "baby" of God's love with the "bathwater" of bad doctrine.

Moving Back to Mainstream

It was going to be so hard for so many of them for so many reasons. One friend of mine put it this way: "When WCG went 'mainstream,' and I saw everything my Daddy and his family had sacrificed for, go right back into a belief system my Dad, and thousands of others had turned their backs on, I was basically done."

She meant done with what we call "religion." But I know this lady. She's got one of the biggest hearts of Christian love I know. She was done with "church." And so were so many.

Still, not all of us were "done." So, pastors who remained had quite a task ahead. The shepherding task was massive, and there weren't a lot of shepherds for us shepherds personally and successfully experienced in the tasks they were giving us to do.

There would be some who simply would not only *not* grasp the changes but who would not even give them a chance. "No way!" they in effect declared, "There's no way we could have been wrong all those centuries" (even though it had only been decades, unless you're playing the Anglo-Israeli card)! With righteous indignation, they'd add, "We've lived this way forever. God has blessed us! We refuse to accept this Satan-inspired misinterpretation of Scripture." And then they'd find ways of continuing to uphold their worldviews and form different splinter groups or associations living in much smaller communities than they used to live in before.

But there were many who were saying that if it's not about keeping Sabbaths and Holy Days, what is it all about? How do we now channel our fervor to continue to serve him? We knew we still wanted to be a church. Many had reaped the benefits of God's Presence in our faith journey. Our spirits were willing to exchange the elemental shadows of this created order (Colossians 2:16-17) for life in the Reality that was Christ.[*]

However, our flesh was still weak. We continued to keep old ways for a long time, but after a point, they began to lose their glow.

---

[*] Therefore do not let anyone judge you by what you eat or drink, or with regard to a religious festival, a New Moon celebration or a Sabbath day. **17 These are a shadow** of the things that were to come; the **reality**, however, **is** found in **Christ**. (emphasis mine) (Colossians 2:16-17)

A Recollection of a Revised Worldview October 2000

It is early fall, and once again I'm on the road with my family, heading south. My wife and my one daughter (the other two will be joining us later), are heading to our traditional worship celebration. We have changed its name, though. We no longer call it the Festival of Tabernacles. We call it Festival 2000: A Celebration of Christ. The theme is evangelism. We'll be having classes during the Festival and will learn how to share Christ with others. We'll still be expecting about 2,000 people there, because this time of year is still special to many of us. After all, some of them have been doing something like this in the fall since they were born.

We're driving through West Virginia now, nestled in the mountains and rolling hills, and it is late at night. Overhead hangs what we used to call the Festival Moon, but I guess I'll start referring to it as Hunter's Moon now. It is beautiful—so large and looming, and it does create a special moment for me, bounded on either side by dimly lit mountains that cradle my path into the night. But I'm more perplexed than awed, a little confused, and maybe even burdened with a bit of righteous angst. How did I ever get to the point that my life was governed by days and months and seasons and years? It seems so ancient, so archaic, so primitive, and so elemental. Did I really spend all those years and all that religious energy following the cyclical changes of the night sky? I guess I went into the Bible asking the wrong question—what day I should keep, rather than what Lord I should follow!

I arrive at the celebration strangely depressed, almost wishing I had stayed home. There are so many things we could be working on back there, so many new initiatives we're starting in our local church. I almost feel as if I don't have the time to be here. But I've been asked to come to serve as a worship leader, and the kids are excited. Oh well, I guess we can do one more for old-time's sake.

When I get to the Festival my attitude does begin to revive a little. We worship Christ here considering our newfound discovery of the depth of what he's done; we really do. The songs I've chosen purposely (I'm one of the Festival worship leaders) reflect his presence in our life now, and the life we can have in him now, rather than the one of just "praying, paying, and waiting" for the Millennium, when we formerly thought we'd finally become teachers and priests. We're learning here that we can become teachers and priests right now, helping people by showing them the access they have to heaven <u>now</u> through a Christ who is alive.

I lead them in a chant that would become my signature worship call for a long time. It's called the "Victory Chant"[23] and people echo these phrases I sing in a singsong chanting style.

If the Greek Orthodox priest could hear me now!

Hail Jesus, You're my king.

Your life frees me to sing.

I will praise you all my days.

You're perfect, in all your ways.

Hail Jesus, You're my lord.

I will obey your word.

I want to see your kingdom come.

Not my will but yours be done.

Glory, glory to the lamb!

You take me into the land.

We will conquer in your name!

And proclaim that Jesus reigns.

God is taking us into the land—now! As Jesus said, the Kingdom of God is in us, and we are in the Kingdom of God. We don't just have to wait for the Wonderful World Tomorrow, as we used to call the Millennium that would rule the world after Christ's return. We can begin conquering in Jesus's name now. We can follow him on Earth as we do in heaven. One person, one family at a time, we can do battle for the Lord like King David. We can advance the Kingdom of God. We can conquer in His name.

It used to be that I didn't want to go home from the Festival. It was almost as if I lived to be here. Now, even though I've come to enjoy it and am glad I came, I can't wait to get home and start putting these principles into practice. I hope that next year they will make this opportunity more user-friendly, so that more folks from back home who can't or won't take their kids out of school to come in the fall, will be able to have access to this great information we're learning about in sharing and celebrating Christ. In fact, they've already announced they're going to host another Festival next summer for that very reason. I'm looking forward to being there.

It's funny how things change. I still looked forward to the denominational gatherings, but instead of spending loads of money on lavish insular fellowship, at this point I became more excited about going back home to share the abundant life of Christ with others. I wanted to live in Christ more fully and show others how to do the same. I was transitioning from a cult to the world of Evangelicalism.

I had been a Christian in a cult, and now I was an Evangelical Christian.

It would take an amazing amount of blood, sweat, tears, and prayer, because we had to continue to free people from wrong approaches to Christ in the past. But we had so much joy in discovering our chance to share Jesus, you would have thought we invented him.

Chapter 11

THE AGONY AND THE ECSTASY –

A BORN AGAIN WCG CHURCH

When a church is trapped in its culture, don't expect things to change overnight. It took us a good five to seven years just to wrap our minds around our doctrinal changes, much less even try to implement them.

Now that I've had to biblically—and with hard-lived experience—take on embedded cultic behaviors and help a congregation truly function as Christians in Christ, I'm warning you: if you're ever faced with something similar, change is going to be hard. And it will expose a lot of things about your organization, and about yourself, that will prove to be greater growth areas than you ever realized.

Such changes might necessitate the dismantling of a religious empire. I mentioned the acceptance of WCG by Evangelical church leaders after "the changes." The epitome of our newly celebrated status was Ruth Tucker's *Christianity Today* article in 1996 called "From the Fringe to the Fold."[24] This was followed by our eventual acceptance into the ranks of the Evangelical Churches of America, the ECA. In our minds, we were now part of a movement within broader Evangelicalism that could help turn Christianity back into a society-transforming movement. This was a huge relief. We were accepted. We were legitimate. This was an antidote against the shame we had felt for being so wrong.

However, if you noticed at the end of the last chapter, the Old Testament military imagery of taking enemy territory for the Kingdom, while directed differently, was still very much alive.

This begs the question that will remain before us as we pick up the narrative. How much of this embattled mentality fed into our new Evangelicalism and how much did Evangelicalism's articulation of winning others into Christ feed into our old ways of thinking? Perhaps more than we realized? Quite a lot I'm afraid, because at the bottom both are based on dividing humanity into an "us vs them." I didn't realize it at the time, but I was now entering my third cult, or "us vs them" culture as I'm using the word here, the "cult" of Evangelicalism.

The Agony

After the changes we went through what seemed like a long, sometimes painful, transition period. For some years after I began my new assignment in Dayton, Ohio in 1999 (four years after the "changes"), the churches were still keeping old days side by side with new ones.

Old habits die hard. I remember the last year we kept a typical Days of Unleavened Bread Holy Day, which the Hebrews were commanded to note with a sacred assembly (Leviticus 23:8).

This year, it happened on a Saturday, convenient for us because we were still going to church on Saturday at that time. But this particular year it so happened the next day was Easter. So (gulp), with fear, trepidation, a little anxiety, but also a little anticipation, we got the nerve to hold a traditional Easter service, even though not so terribly long ago we would have seen that as the apex of worshipping God with paganism. And we did it . . . hold your breath . . . on a Sunday, no less! For us, that was an amazing new experience, since we'd been so conditioned for so long to keep a Saturday Sabbath and it simply did not yet feel right going to church on Sunday.

On Easter of all days! We were still cognizant of all those easily searchable references on the web about how this was somehow really the festival of "Astarte" and laced with all kinds of pagan roots.* We had been conditioned to disdain days in any way based on such roots for so long. Yet, as we just so recently learned, all things had been made new in Christ (2 Corinthians 5:17)! And that included even all days that were formerly claimed by the pagans. We could use *any day*---even a formerly "pagan" day---to proclaim the centrality

---

* This is why I almost cringe in physical repulsion when I hear some of the "logic" conspiracy theory adherents are coming up with these days. Forgive me for saying this, they simply don't know just how embarrassingly illogical some of their logic sounds, especially to someone who has been there and done that.

of Christ and what he did for us in his death and resurrection. The pagans didn't own any of the days of the week! Christ owned them all! So we could reclaim them in Christ's name, and use them for the expansion of *his* kingdom!

Just as Paul used the "idol" of the unknown god to proclaim the true God (Acts 17:23), we could use pagan things to proclaim the real God and His son Jesus Christ. So, we did! That Easter, we used a formerly "pagan" event to proclaim the true God and His Son Jesus Christ.

And God unmistakably blessed it.

Following Spirit and Scripture

The aliveness of the latter service stood in sharp contrast to the humdrum Sabbath service the day before. The presence of the Spirit, the joy, and even the presence of new people coming for the first time to our church told many of us one thing: it was time to let go of the old and step into the new. The celebration exhibited too much of the Presence of the Spirit to be ignored. The crowd was twice the size of our normal attendance. It didn't hurt that I, ever the son of Greek food festival traditions, had the insight to suggest that we also provide a lunch of Greek lamb afterward.

With that start, we began to live out the Victory Chant. We began to "conquer" in Christ's name. One block, one street at a time. And, again, we sought to do this simplistically, from our hearts, still looking to the Bible to show us what to do, Jesus style.

I went to Scripture for the next scenes in the drama of our little ministry's life. The first one we saw was this: before Jesus began his ministry, he fasted for forty days. So, we began a late summer initiative called Forty Days of Prayer and Fasting that we used to discern God's vision for us for our next year's activities. This is how it flowed:

- Invite at least one person to sign up for each of the forty days in the designated period.
- Come together and share what God had shared with us.
- Put together a shared vision from the discerned steps.

It became an annual event for a long time. Many wonderful new initiatives emanated from that for several years.

It was after the First 40 Days of Prayer and Fasting that we finally and officially cut the cord with Saturday worship services. Just like Paul would go to wherever the people were to preach the Gospel and make it accessible, we were going to go to what was the culturally preferable worship day for the world culture in which we lived. That was undoubtedly Sunday. We set the date, held our breath, and *finally* took the plunge.

After that first year, Easter became a special marker for us. It was as if the Lord had risen especially for us in *our* first Easter service in more ways than one. They were amazing days of joy as we sincerely and simplistically reveled in the story of Jesus.

It's Not About the Numbers

Since we'd just had our doctrinal resurrection, it seemed to us locally the logical thing to do was to join Jesus and the early church in the Acts 1 experience, which occurred after Christ's literal resurrection. The Bible, and our resurrection experience, were just that real for us in at least our little corner of the WCG world. We were nearing our own first Pentecost where we knew (or at least hoped) the Lord was going to send us the numbers.

But as time went on, we realized that numbers could be misleading. Pentecost numbers are nice, but more important are habits of spiritual formation and disciple-making. Jesus had healed thousands, opened the eyes of the blind, healed the lame, raised the dead, taught amazing things, died, and topped it all off with the resurrection. But even after all that, he was still just left with about 120 praying people when all was said and done (Acts 1:15).

If you study it closely, Jesus had a lot of expansions and contractions in the number of followers throughout his ministry. Some contractions he seemed to initiate intentionally. Jesus would do "off-the-wall" things that would often shock his disciples and attract large crowds. But then he would thin the mega crowd who followed Him down to more manageable, smaller, and spiritually hungry numbers. Look at what took place after the feeding of the 5,000. This event was such a crowd-pleaser, he had people crossing lakes in small boats just to be with him the next day.

But darn it if Jesus failed to leverage this big crowd moment and keep the momentum going. Interestingly, he did quite the opposite. He appeared to insult the crowd's motives the very next day (John 6:26) followed by what I'm sure at least some disciples thought was a disastrous sermon that sounded as if he was teaching both the eating of unclean food and downright cannibalism.

Jesus told the people who had taken this day off and all those who had followed him in boats that they were not after God's will or God's work. He told them that they just wanted more bread and the magic bullet of continual physical provision. They wanted an Old Testament version of health and wealth religion, for physical manna to rain down from Heaven (John 6:25-27). In other words, they were simply following him to get more free groceries!

Then, to top it all off, instead of giving an easy-to-access Five Easy Steps to Succeed at Getting Free Food (or whatever) from God's message, he started getting too theological. Rather than saying something easy to understand, and possibly offering a brief reference to Scripture, he simply strung together one seemingly inexplicable mystical saying after another.

> *I am the living bread that came down from heaven. Whoever **eats** this bread will live forever. This bread is **my flesh**, which I will give for the life of the world."* [emphasis mine] (John 6:51)

> *Whoever **eats my flesh** and **drinks my blood** has eternal life, and I will raise them up at the last day.* [emphasis mine] (John 6:54)

> *Whoever **eats my flesh** and **drinks my blood** remains in me, and I in them.* [emphasis mine] (John 6:56)

He was saying this to Jews who wouldn't even be in the same room with a ham sandwich, much less consider eating human flesh and, of all things—blood! Hadn't he read Deuteronomy 12:23?

He was obviously taking them to the next level. They had just tried to come and make him an earthly king after the miraculous feeding. To them, this was the health and wealth Gospel come true (John 6:15). But after a night of prayer, he knew what he had to do (John 6:14, Matthew 14:23). He had to get their mind off the physical bread and put it on the spiritual bread. To the disciples' chagrin, he seized defeat out of the jaws of victory.

And he lost the crowds! Doggone it, he lost the crowds! He could draw them in, but he couldn't keep them. In John 6:66 it states the damaging impact this had on Jesus' ministry:

From that time many of his disciples turned back and no longer followed him.
(John 6:66)

In the original Greek, it infers that they went back to the things "they left behind." *

Even the 12 were confused.

"You do not want to leave too, do you?" he asked them.
(John 6:68)

Simon Peter answered him:

"Lord, to whom shall we go? You have the words of eternal life. We have come to believe and know that you are the Holy One of God!" (John 6:69)

Translation—we've got no idea what you're talking about half the time, but we "know" (feel) God in your presence, even in your words. We're still here!

Lessons Learned about Christ and "Crowds"

But this was the lesson to me. Even Jesus didn't keep everybody. He'd have expansions in the crowds, and then contractions in the size of the crowds that followed him. We would too. One of the first (and most painful) things we had to get used to after the changes was people who had been with us prior to our doctrinal changes leaving. Even if you tried to chase down these "lost" (or leaving) sheep, they'd still leave. So, we got used to people leaving. And working in the market-driven world of Evangelicalism was no different. People would still come and go. Especially if we did things Jesus often did— not just give the cultural crowd-pleasing things they demanded but the things Christ gave his disciples as he was growing his movement.

In other words, I felt Christ was saying two things to me:

- Don't just make this "Bible lite" to attract and keep the crowds who simply refuse to go deeper.

---

* One of the nuances of the word *opiso* used here is to go back to the "things left behind." Consider that in light of 2 Peter 2:21 (emphasis mine): It would have been better for them not to have known the way of righteousness, *than to have known it and then to turn their backs on the sacred command that was passed on to them.*

- And don't feel so bad when people come and go.

We used scenes like this to comfort ourselves with our relatively small numbers (about 70-ish at the time). We did set a growth goal for a church of about 120, but our study of Scripture encouraged us to prioritize the creation of smaller groups of devout people who wanted to go deeper before wider. If we lost focus, the size of the crowd might become an end to itself, and people would find themselves talking more about the numbers they attracted than about Jesus.

We also received from Acts 1 another early initiative. We needed to replace lost leadership (in their case, Judas, in ours, people and ministry leaders who scattered after the changes). So, we focused on rebuilding new leaders. We made an intentional choice to include in our leadership some of our most enthusiastic early adopters—our Worldwide Church of God (WCG) young people.

But it came with a price.

WCG – We Camp Good; WCB – We Carry Baggage

We had managed to retain at least some of our young people in the early days of our transition. They had formed wonderful life alliances in their shared experiences of being a culture within a culture. They'd bonded rather intensely in shared alternative youth sports activities the church provided. In particular, they bonded in what had turned out to be a high-quality, powerful summer camp program called the Summer Educational Program (SEP) that many of our young people participated in. It was run by a skilled professional who had both leadership gifts and effectiveness in reaching young people.

It occurred to some that it was one of our remaining strengths—a still-glowing ember in a rapidly dying fire. These young people were still with us and still wanted to participate in our camp (later to become camps). And by continuing to provide a regional camp program, some in the denomination hoped to provide a place where eager, zealous, evangelical young people would take the reins from a worship-weary aging pastoral pool[*] and raise a new era of leaders for the denomination, phoenix-like from the ashes of the old.

---

[*] Filled with "old dogs" who apparently couldn't or wouldn't learn new tricks, or so it was perceived by some.

Frankly, that made a lot of sense to me. When Israel escaped Egypt, it was the old guys that had to die out and those under twenty who would go into the Promised Land (my euphemism for life in the evangelical world of the New Covenant). Some of our most productive young supporters seemed to be capable of bearing positive fruit for our local church. Many of my pastoral peers were not jumping eagerly into outreach approaches. But at any rate, I bought in—at least partially. I became an early adopter of empowering young people to have prominent roles in the next generation of our churches. But it came with a price, one that would manifest later. Like anyone whose capacity of choice has been overly repressed, these young people came with some cult-induced baggage as well. This included their over-realized expectation of what they would be able to accomplish.* But for now, I'll continue to share what it was like during what I refer to as the true golden age of our reformation.

The Ecstasy

For a while, we were all in a honeymoon phase. We'd all gotten on the same page. We wanted to survive. We still figured God had a purpose for all we'd been through. We'd negotiated the changes together. We shared common prayer initiatives. We saw God bless our early efforts to sincerely move forward. We were even encouraged by the initial training support we received from the denomination encouraging outreach. We were all at least trying to get dressed up and ready to go.

We adopted a one-on-one mentoring program. We discovered that newly baptized members benefited immensely by connecting to older, more seasoned members. Momentum began to build. This one-on-one mentoring worked, and relationships were built.

We focused on the discovery of spiritual gifts. Spiritual gifts were assessed and "unwrapped." People started putting their God-given endowments to work for the church. By 2015 a ministry team comprised of practically all newer members had been formed. We met monthly and worked together to cast dreams and visions for the church's next steps.

Special events became outreach events. Members enthusiastically brought friends and family. We no longer overly emphasized keeping days and months

---

* Young people don't become "Timothy's" without the aggressive hands-on example of older "Apostle Paul" types leading the way. It seemed to me key leaders had hopes that wouldn't have to be the case. But my experience taught me differently.

and seasons and years. We were no longer simply "keeping days" rather than hosting some in-house peak events. People were coming! Things were beginning to move forward. It was time to replant our ministry in a new location. And Jesus seemed to be leading us—every step of the way.

Picking a New Name for Our Church

It came time to rename our local congregation with a more personalized name than just the name of the denomination. The name CrossRoads seemed to fit us. It seemed to have a dual connotation for the people who had been a part of this church even from the "old" days. For one, we'd learned that Jesus was indeed the "crossroads" —the true intersection of God and humanity. We had just discovered him, and we were like a freshly blinded-by-the-light apostle Paul. He himself had been formerly zealous for the Jewish laws. We had too. But he, too, learned it was all about Jesus in a dramatic sort of way (Acts 8). We'd both graduated from being simply zealous for the law to being zealous for Jesus.

There was another reason the name "crossroads" fit these people. These legacy members were the people of the "plain truth." Whenever they believed God was leading them to a crossroads of change, they'd take it. When they thought God wanted them to keep the Sabbath, they'd even lose jobs to keep the Sabbath. But even more miraculously, when they learned God *didn't* require the Sabbath, and that community outreach and evangelism would work better with a Sunday morning service, they'd switch. Many, many people left WCG after the changes, but it is truly remarkable how many followed the leadership into the new paradigm.

We were people of the crossroads. We had followed what we perceived as God's revelation through his servant HWA (our name for Herbert W. Armstrong), but God brought us to a crossroads of change necessitated by new revelation under new leadership. So, CrossRoads became the church's name. And God was about to take us into an even newer crossroads. God was about to give a group of people who'd always only rented meeting spaces for their services something they never had before. God was about to give us a building. And in the way it happened, this building truly came from God.

Chapter 12

A PINNACLE OF EVANGELICALISM

By what I consider purely the hand of God, we were able to purchase a building. This was a huge deal for us, because for years, our denomination had been against the purchase of buildings. There were reasons given that I honestly can't remember. But my gut tells me that, as much as anything, it was for financial reasons. Local building ownership would have deflected funds locally more than a "headquarters" focused denomination would prefer. But by and large, the leadership (some more than others) was now open to it, so it was quite a move for us to take a big bold step and consider buying a building.

A small building owned by the Catholic Church a few blocks down the street came up for sale. It had a beautiful 100-year-old chapel and a detached but functioning activity center. At first, it was priced at $500,000. That was way over our budget. It went down and, eventually, the asking price was dropped to $330,000. It was still high for us, but with the $50,000 we had managed to set aside in our checking account, we decided to step out in faith and make an offer. Maybe we could make it work with some contingencies. We would lease/option to buy for five years, get the price owed on the building down to $250,000, and then if our ministry took off, we'd buy the building. Even with our contingency plan, it would have been a stretch. Meanwhile, our zealous prayer warrior said she'd been praying to God that if this was the right building, to let the price come down another $100,000.

The real estate agent came back with an offer he'd never had before. The Catholic Church board had decided that they would drop the price $80,000 (from $330,000), and if we could come up with a $250,000 loan now, the building was ours. We figured $80,000 was close enough to the $100,000 our prayer lady prayed for, and with fresh God-backed confidence, we accepted their counteroffer.

We got a loan, and the building appraised so well that we did not have to spend any of our money on a down payment. We used the money we did have to build what we lovingly called "The Connector." This was a walkway that connected the two buildings so folks could walk back and forth between them without having to go outside. As it turned out, the distance between the buildings allowed for just enough of a slope to meet standards considered acceptable for wheelchair passage. It seemed to us God's fingerprints were all over this move. And the concept of making "connections" would prove to be a seminal one for us in the years to come.

The Jesus of John – Walking, Talking, Praying, Calling

Blessed with a building anchored right in the middle of Tipp City, Ohio, we set out to live lives of salt and light, and to do what Jesus did. We were determined to leave the insular ways of the Old Covenant and to be more outward-looking. Just as most of Jesus' earthly ministry centered within the walking circumference of Galilee, we set out to get to know our neighbors. As we studied the book of John together, we noted that as Jesus met people he would talk to them, challenge them, and inspire them on a soul-to-soul level. Quite often the encounter would end up in a call of some sort.

We began to "call" people who we met in our community. In one sense it looked like inviting them to church. More than that, I often felt God guiding me into a conversation that would lead to some sort of spiritual moment with these people before they ever arrived at the church. This was an attempt to follow the example of Jesus in John 1, who was able to tell Nathaniel, "When you were under the fig tree, I saw you." It caused such a response in Nathaniel that he became a follower of Christ (John 1:47-49). I was amazed at how often God gave me just the insights I needed to engage people in spiritual moments in public places where we crossed paths. It only further piqued their curiosity. When Sunday morning rolled around, there they were.

We found the Jesus of John to be creative and provocative, and unafraid to challenge the social barriers of his time. We see a model of this in his seemingly intentional encounter with the Samaritan woman at the well. The story showed how Jesus also knew the value of doing the "off the wall" unexpected thing. First, he spoke to a Samaritan. Jews just didn't do that. Even more shockingly, this Samaritan was a *woman*. That was so off the wall, even his disciples were amazed. And to top it off, he asked to drink from her ladle. For a Jew to do this with a Samaritan might be the equivalent of a racist white American sharing a plate of food and the same fork with a Black person in the Jim Crow South. Jesus showed that he did not fit the mold of the typical Jew or the typical Rabbi, and while doing so he redefined our understanding of God and humanity.

I love the book of John. In it, Jesus seems to speak "God" but people hear "human." He's always saying things over their heads. In this story, he managed to guide a conversation that, at first, began with a simple request for water and in the end transcended the woman's physical perceptions to open her up to spiritual ones.

Combined with our study of John, we'd heard the phrase "what would Jesus do?" and we began using it as a motto of sorts. But we eventually came to see that it wasn't just doing what Jesus did. It was about joining him in WIJD— what is Jesus doing *now*? And it seemed that Jesus was doing a lot in our ministry, opening doors, blessing it to truly engage and call and baptize. Virtually yearly, and often throughout the year, we baptized those who followed Jesus' call.

Bringing New People to Christ—an Unprecedented Joy

Our church was still composed mainly of old members—excuse me—long-time members who'd been in the old church and kept the old ways. We came to call them legacy members because it sounded better than just calling them "old." These old or legacy members weren't just old in age either. Frankly, our demographic was pretty much spread out among younger and older people. At first, they were mostly legacy members, but slowly yet surely new people began to come.

These people were not just church transfers. Someone had told me that church transfer growth isn't authentic kingdom growth anyway. It's just "sheep shuffling"—sheep called to another flock, getting bored (primarily with their "shepherd" or pastor), and shuffling off to new pastors and new approaches. I actually sent one lady frustrated with her own pastor and looking for a new church back to her old one to work things out with her pastor. It was tough to do so. Growth was still slow, and having a new person become a part of us would have been very encouraging. But it was heartbreaking enough for me when many of our legacy members began to leave us, freed doctrinally from not "having" to be in what was no longer God's only "one true church." I didn't want to do that to someone else.

An unprecedented joy was when God allowed me, an ex-cult pastor, to be used to bring people to Christ who had never come to him before. Baby boomers who'd become disenchanted with religion at an early age during the days of the Vietnam War and the sexual revolution came to Christ. A young professional whose life had lost meaning came to Christ. There was the lady with whom I stopped to chat by her hedges and entered a friendly conversation. Little did I know she was holding a tall glass of some alcoholic beverage in her hand that she deftly hid in the bushes when I approached her! She came to church, restarted AA, and came to Christ and got baptized.

Again, I could not tell you how many I baptized. Maybe 200-plus. I remember praying this blessing early on in our reformation: "May God use us to bring hundreds and thousands and millions to Christ." God had answered the first part of the prayer. We'd at least started with the "hundreds" part.

Some would say it was clear God had not cured me of my epic tendencies! We unapologetically had our belief in a big God, and a profound sense of a new understanding of what he might do in us and through us as we sought to follow him. Scripture is full of little people with big dreams and big asks who have seen God do amazing things. We wanted to be in that number. So, with no road map to follow and no mentor to lead, we took our cues from the Bible as if it applied to us personally. As my approach to the Christ of the New Covenant began to grow, so did I.

An important distinction came to mind at this time. We not only could do things *for* Jesus but also *with* him. Actually, it was more than that. We could simply let him do his "thing" in us. I now knew that we could not only see Jesus and copy him, we could be a new presentation of him as he lived his life in and through us. Illuminated by the Spirit, we could "re" present him, not just "represent" him. And the Spirit moved mightily in our midst; new believers packed the Wednesday night class about the book of Acts we called "First Church." People were fascinated at how vibrant life in Christ could be.

At the Cross Service—a New Way to Keep Good Friday

Since we rediscovered the biblical legitimacy of celebrating the key events of Christ's ministry with Christmas and Easter, we kept them as if we had just invented them. We kept them with the wonder of a child at her first Christmas. We created whole new traditions for these 2,000-year-old worship events, and they were uniquely beautiful.

A highlight of the Easter season was our At the Cross Service. Traditionally, Maundy Thursday services rehearse Jesus' Last Supper and host a special evening communion, often with some form of reenactment of the foot-washing Jesus did that night. On Good Friday, people remembered Jesus' crucifixion and death in various ways. We connected the two, added elements of our Old Covenant Passover service with some new elements of Good Friday, and combined them into one event. This internal connection reminded us that the New Covenant did not *replace* the Old Covenant, but revealed what the *one* Covenant really was all about.

We began the service with an audience-participation rehearsal of the Last Supper. We'd cook and serve portions of lamb Mediterranean style and as authentically as we could discern. (It was a Greek recipe, but the *Amerikáni*, Greek in-house jargon for Americans who, sadly, weren't blessed to be Greek* wouldn't know the difference.) We'd add olives, cheese, dried Middle Eastern fruits, and other items we imagined Jesus might have had at his table. We even threw in the green onions I remembered Abraham and Sarah served God and the angels in the arched mural at the Birmingham Greek Orthodox Church.

We started this service dinner theatre style in the fellowship hall, which had been converted into the Upper Room where all the preparations had been made ready according to the Gospel accounts. Participants played the role of a guest at Jesus' Last Supper. We'd introduce the evening, let them engage in the meal, and interrupt it dramatically—just as we thought Jesus did with the foot washing. We demonstrated the foot washing, spoke of the betrayal of Judas, and rehearsed the introduction of the first communion. With the lights lowered and candles aglow, we took the bread and the wine with great reverence. And then we would dramatically interrupt the flow with a depiction of the arrest of Jesus. Our goal was not just to talk about it or read about it. It was to help us all *experience* the moment when Jesus was arrested. We wanted to help people feel what it was like to be there when they crucified our Lord.

---

* I really am just joking . . . sort of!

103

We dramatized Judas taking the bread and leaving and then we turned off the lights to depict the darkness that was settling in as Jesus was arrested and later beaten.

Then we'd adjourn to the sanctuary where candles lit the lonely cross, which was placed front and center. We'd do what we said was the opposite of what the first disciples did that night. Instead of leaving him alone and fleeing from the cross, we'd stay and worship him *at* the cross. In our holy imagination, we tried to feel an iota of his suffering even as he felt all of ours. We worshiped him and thanked him for it, and we challenged ourselves. We asked ourselves if we were like Peter throughout most of the year. Are we, too, following him "at a distance" when it comes time for the cross? Or did we have the bravery like John to follow him by choosing to stay with him "at the cross," not desert him there, and to live with him "in" the way of the cross?

It was a wonderful, meaningful almost liturgical service. Members would spend hours decorating, preparing, cooking, and serving. One service someone spent the night before at the building, roasting a whole lamb and readying for the service to honor Jesus. We were all inspired. We had the sense God was creating something new through us.

Christmas Candle Lighting Service

When you don't have holiday traditions in your church, the imagination is free to indulge. The Christmas Candle Lighting Service was another new (to us) celebration that soon everyone, not just the kids, looked forward to every year. The Sunday before Christmas was always an evening service. We'd call it Sleep-In-Sunday because we'd not hold the morning service that day. The service climaxed as the early sunset of winter darkened the chapel. We'd conclude by lighting candles and singing "Silent Night, Holy Night" and encouraging all to keep a wonderful Christmas in simple fashion, with their families and God---like Jesus did, the first Christmas---and to experience a little rest and "reboot" in him. We did this in lieu of services on Christmas Eve or Christmas morning, specifically so people *could be home* those times *with their loved ones*, the way Jesus was with his, at *his* "first" Christmas.

It was an unforgettable service. We were truly being transformed by this season. To me, it connected the best of all our history: the biblical passion for serving God "extra" on "high" (especially holy) days, and the joy of discovering the Incarnation of Christ as the center of all history, his-tory, or *his* "story," which is our "story" too.

We realized we weren't to just read about the Incarnation. We were supposed to live it in our communities as well. So, we did.

The community became aware of our church in part because, like Jesus, we made an intentional effort to *connect with* the community. The Jesus of John went to secular events like the wedding at Cana and the love of God was made manifest in action. Likewise, we intentionally put our tentacles out to connect with any agency doing good work in the community. Even if they were not giving credit where credit was due for their good work, we could!

Thinking of the Jesus of John, I personally committed to spend more time connecting people to people and people to resources. I soon found myself on the United Way board of directors and gained invaluable public relations collateral for the church by serving on it. In a way I found myself shepherding folks who didn't even come to our church. We were all learning a lifestyle where we could spread the love of Jesus wherever we went, and make connections in his name, connecting real needs, good deeds, and people from all walks of life. More weekends than not, I was in the town's Saturday morning market on a downtown street, helping and simply meeting people there too, hopefully, having some meaningful conversations in the name of Christ.

Commuter Church to Community Church

The church began to grow. We were never a mega-church. It was micro by today's standards. We almost, but not quite, broke the 100 barrier for regular attendance. But now the majority of our congregation were "new" people from the local community. People were happy. There was a new enthusiasm for inviting people to church and winning people to Christ. Young adults started to fill the pews, and some were interested in pastoral ministry. I was hoping that we could possibly plant churches in other areas and help the denomination fulfill its dream of becoming a church-planting movement.

In 2015, we even got this notice of recognition from the social media facilitator at LifeWay Christian Resources.[25]

> *James and Becky Valekis have been at Crossroads Christian Fellowship since 1999, when James became the senior pastor there. Crossroads is a "re-birthed" congregation, and the church has been experiencing a significant amount of change over the last 10 or 15 years since the Valekises arrived, so they decided it was time to do some self-assessment.*

105

Crossroads Christian Fellowship is part of Grace Communion International (GCI), a denomination present in over 70 countries and made up of over 50,000 members in about 900 churches. One spring, GCI leadership recommended LifeWay Research's Transformational Church Assessment Tool (TCAT) to churches who may benefit from assessing themselves and moving forward in ministry effectiveness.

Pastor Valekis and Crossroads did some research, contacted LifeWay Research, and embarked on their journey of self-assessment.

Since the arrival of Pastor Valekis in 1999, Crossroads found themselves transitioning from a more commuter-based congregation to a more traditional, community-based congregation.

Becky, Pastor Valekis' wife and a leader in the church, said, "We started there [Crossroads] in 1999-2000, and we were 100 percent commuter-based, I would guess. Then, by the time we did the TCAT last year, we were probably more like 80 percent community based."

That's a huge demographic swing. Such a change would have no small effect on the congregation.

The transition was a big one, and the church thought some self-assessment would go a long way in helping them better minister to the community around them.

They were right.

Crossroads, Mrs. Valekis says, actually scored really well on the TCAT. But, while there were no glaring areas needing improvement, the assessment confirmed a suspicion many in leadership had: communication could improve, specifically as it relates to the mission and vision of the church and its discipleship efforts.

The question the leadership faced is this: "How do we improve our communication with the congregation?"

Pastor Valekis, Mrs. Valekis, and other leaders in the church found a solution: more leadership.

"One of the things that came out of it [the assessment] was that we really did need more leadership, to spread out more. So we've been working on creating a more varied leadership structure, and we just commissioned and ordained three new leaders since the assessment," Mrs. Valekis reported.

Pastor Valekis is the only full-time pastor of Crossroads, so other part-time and lay leaders to assist him have done wonders to bring about communication effectiveness in the church. Church members can contact any number of church leaders now, instead of relying on Pastor Valekis to be available.

The expansion of leadership is already starting to show fruit. Crossroads is a church of approximately 80 regular attenders, and Mrs. Valekis says that since they've commissioned the new leaders, attendance has been up, and they just recently baptized 17 people on a single Sunday!

Crossroads is experiencing a renaissance of sorts, with increasing attendance, increasing interest in baptism and church involvement, and significant financial giving. Mrs. Valekis sees taking the TCAT as a sort of turning point for the church.

"We were at a good place, but we didn't know what the next step was. So I think that it's helped us see that a little bit better," she said.

As the report testifies, Becky was an amazing partner in ministry. We were in a good place. It was fresh. It was original. It wasn't cookie-cutter. It was fruitful. But it only lasted "one brief shining moment." Just as the mythical Camelot met a tragic end, so did CrossRoads. Both, it seemed, were too good to be true. For all that we were Christians in Christ, we still had our "cults" to negotiate.

Specifically, there were three cultic strands. The first one was the "ex-cult" backdrop of the Armstrong culture from which we sprang, trying (but not always succeeding) to reform in function as well as doctrine. The second strand was my own "cultic" expectations and baggage (that went way back to my childhood rearing in the culture of the Greek Orthodox faith), exacerbated by the shared growing pains that come from being part of a recovering ex-cult. But the most surprising was the third strand, which many of us are passively a part of without realizing it. That is the cultic "us vs them" theology of Evangelicalism.

The "us versus them" in the Evangelical world was not based on 1) reverence to a "cult leader" (although sometimes pastor-centric churches can scarily reflect that). And it was not 2) the ethnically oriented superiority complex of my Greek upbringing. It wasn't either of these, but it had elements of both.

The one true church mindset of Evangelicalism thrives on the "us" vs "them" construct. In my experience, even if it wasn't ethnic superiority, there was a built-in superiority with a mindset that said "we are in" with Christ and "you are out."

The focal point was not usually on an individual cult leader, but it *was* based on an isolated individual, Jesus Christ (without the Trinitarian context), and it was pitched to people who are viewed as individuals isolated from Christ. Instead of being the Savior of all people (1 Timothy 4:10), Jesus was my Savior and brother *only if I as an individual asked him to be.*

This exclusion-before-inclusion approach was meant to motivate us to evangelize the heathen. The idea was to go take Christ to others *because he wasn't there.* Go win people to Christ because they did not belong to him. Run summer Bible camps and get people to make "a decision" to invite Christ into their lives, because otherwise their hearts are "God-shaped vacuums." This is the insular "cultic" expression of the modern-day American Evangelical landscape.

By starting potential converts out in the category of "them"—*they* who were separated from God until *they* did something—I was feeding the restlessness I now see that many Evangelicals must feel deep down. The angst goes something like this: "If *my* decision connected me with God, how do I know if *I* did it right enough, and for the right motives? Was I truly sincere? I know a good tree only bears good fruit (Matthew 7:17), but since baptism, my actions have not always been consistent with Christ. Oh my, maybe I'm not one of "us" after all, but one of "them" (the bad trees)!"

At our pinnacle at CrossRoads we succeeded in getting many people to church, many across the threshold to Christ. "Multitudes" (from my limited perspective and within the context of our doctrinally reformed world) were baptized. But we had difficulty growing Christians to true depth and maturity. Perhaps this was founded in the same restlessness that plagued me. My ministry became more conflicted and entangled as I dimly began to grow in Trinitarian approaches. "You can bring them in," one critic of my ministry observed rather disrespectfully in a public setting over which I was presiding, "but you can't keep them!" And he was right! I would bring them in using the Evangelical playbook but try to keep them assuming they'd naturally gravitate to Trinitarian concepts later. Evangelicalism fed the control mechanisms ingrained within me by my cult days, making God's love *conditional* on what we do (we are God's beloved children *only if* we make a decision). But as of yet I was unequipped to disciple believers in the context of a gospel of *unconditional* love. Where was the accountability to live for Christ?

The three cultic strands of my now "Evangelical" life twisted around each other and interacted with me and others in such a way that they created a perfect storm.

Chapter 13

CULTS IN COLLISION PART 1: WORKING WITH AN EX-CULT MEMBERSHIP IN OUR LOCAL CHURCH

I f you dare to call out cultic behavior in your church, what can you expect?

I remember a cartoon I saw featuring Garfield the cat by Jim Davis. My friend Tom first introduced me to him. Garfield was at a place where cats were confined to cage-like kennels. In one frame Garfield is shown taking the locks off the doors. He then opens them wide and ebulliently declares "You're free! You're free!" In the next frame, it shows the kenneled cats' unified response. They're frozen and look scared to death. Not one of them has dared walk out of their cages.

In the next strip, the ever-resourceful Garfield adjusts. He closes their cage doors and locks them tight. And then he proclaims to the cats too scared to leave the safety of the kennels: "You're secure! You're secure!"

Surprisingly, that is what it was like for many in our legacy church. Some of our legacy members were like the old wineskins, dried out by years of legalism. Or maybe it's not that they were dried out but rather like memory foam mattresses, they had etched into their collective psyche an imprint of functioning and way of being that was hard to reshape. They had a tough time changing and engaging. They were about as stretched as they could be in the early years of our transition. Adopting new ways of being was too destabilizing. Character regressions occurred. New growth created more losses among old members. Outreach was difficult because, even when people were willing to check us out, the follow-up by members was unpredictable.

The following stories in this chapter illustrate these points.

Why True Worship Days Won't Solve a Problem with Cussing, But How Unlearning Them Might Start One

That's how I entitled a story I wrote in my 2001 graduate thesis "Open the Eyes of My Heart Lord—We Want to See Jesus."

The story was about a man in my congregation in the early years after "the changes." One who had accepted, at least theologically, our transition from Old Covenant approaches toward worship days to New Covenant ones. He made what by then had come to be called "the changes." He had bought into their biblical veracity. But after a while, he was not happy. He was so unsettled by all the unfamiliarity and "freedom" that walking in new ways brought to his life, that he wanted to go back to the old ways. He just wanted to restore some kind of normalcy to his life.

It was not unlike the problem faced by the author of Hebrews, who wrote to Christian Jews drifting their way back into the cultic Temple system of sacrifices. It was so much easier to worship through a system you were used to and could feel and see and could physically find security in by following repeat patterns, than to grow with an unseen Savior who sent his invisible Spirit from heaven. Jesus nailed it when he said:

> *"No one after drinking old wine wants the new, for they say, 'The old is better.'"*
> (Luke 5:39)

Here is how I described the scene in my thesis:

> *One day after a church service, a man approached me with a sense of urgency. He had something he needed to talk about. There was frustration in his voice. His anxiety, discomfort, and insecurity were very real.*
>
> *"We need to sit down and have a long talk," he said. "I've got some things I'm struggling with."*
>
> *"About what?" I asked, wanting to know at least the general direction our conversation was going to take. I did not want to fret with pastoral curiosity until the time the "long talk" could take place.*
>
> *"I don't want to broadside you with this," he said haltingly, probably because of the long-standing tensions regarding the issues he was going to bring up... "Please," I gently insisted. "Tell me at least what it's about."*

111

"I've got to go back," he responded. "I've got to go back to keeping days."

He went on to explain, "I haven't prayed consistently for three years. I'm beginning to cuss again. I don't engage in any of the spiritual disciplines anymore. I've got to go back to doing things like I used to. I've got to go back to keeping days."

"I've got to go back."

He acknowledged that the doctrinal transformation was valid. He acknowledged that at least in theory, moving on to a transforming relationship with Christ rather than a controlling relationship with symbols, was a better place to be. But he also acknowledged how badly he wanted "to go back." It sounded so much to me like the cries the biblical Moses heard from Israelites who wanted to go back to the familiarity of slavery in Egypt, rather than the painful wanderings of a desert journey to freedom (Numbers 11:18-20). It made me wonder if this was what the author of Hebrews was struggling with. I could not help but think about Paul and the pleas he made in his letter to the Galatians. I kept asking myself, "How do you turn again" to these weak and beggarly elements? No wonder Paul used words like "bewitched" when he was talking about this:

"You foolish Galatians! Who has bewitched you?" (Galatians 3:1)[26]

For a pastor attempting to lead a people through a difficult transformation, for one trying to see where even his own life experience fit into all this, this moment stirred some powerful personal feelings. I could not help but note how, for some, the particular symbol system of their religion seemed to be more than just communication tools that they used. They may acknowledge the limitations of them and move away from them as circumstances warrant or permit. But for some, it was as if the symbol system itself became the focus of their religion and the power behind their religion. Since it seems to work so well for them, they eventually feel it should become the ultimate religious expression for all. The outward forms of these symbols are somehow required to evoke the reality of the dynamic undergirding them. They are seen to have so much power, that Christ simply cannot be revealed in fullness without them.

"I can't have Christ without these pointers," one former member wrote me, as she struggled to grasp Pauline attitudes towards worship days and Christianity. Those pointers, her argument went, and those "God-given pointers that come from the Bible alone," are the best ones and really the only ones through which God can reveal the fullness of God.

Of course, the insistence of these "pointers" ushering us into the fullness of God flew in the face of the central precept of Colossians 2:9, that Jesus Christ *directly* is the fullness of God in bodily form. These are just some examples of what we had to face as we attempted to hold together as a group and make the changes it would take to become a New Covenant-based, kingdom-expanding church. When it comes to our choosing between Christ and a comfortable religious culture, Christ often takes a back seat.

Old Dogs, New Tricks, and New Members

As many new people began to attend church, they eventually comprised a sizable part of the worshiping crowd. But not all the former members knew how to respond to that, or apparently even cared.

I'll never forget when a long-time member stood before his pew and announced to me that he was no longer coming to church. His reason was an odd and unexpected reaction to the fact that several new people had started coming in and replacing many of the "old people," undoubtedly some of his friends, who had drifted away.

"I look around here and see nothing but strangers!" he said. "I can go to church with strangers in my own neighborhood!" he added with emphasis. "Why drive here?"

So, he chose not to anymore. Wow. What do you do with that? "Old wineskins" to me were becoming "old whine-skins." Long-time members whined about the loss of members. But now they complained about the growing numbers of new ones.

Again, I guess I can understand the fact that underneath my friend's words was a longing for community. That's a good thing, and one he had enjoyed before the changes. The new people were not "his people," and starting over to build the time-honored relationships necessary for community is very threatening to most.

But for me, it became so confusing. Even when we won, it sometimes felt like we still lost!

Awkward Outreach Backup

As mentioned earlier, I'd begun a fairly successful door-to-door neighborhood outreach ministry. I'd meet people, wait for God to create a shared spiritual moment with them, usually prayer, and often they'd come to church.

One story comes to mind. It was a snowy winter day. I was sitting in the basement of our church watching the snow fall, getting ready for a Sunday service on a Saturday afternoon. I noticed that a plaster repair truck was parked at one of the houses I could see from the window where I was sitting at my desk preparing a sermon. We needed plaster work done in the church, so I chose to seize the moment and be the friendly neighborhood pastor. I figured if Jesus' thirst was part of his motivation for approaching the Samaritan lady, it was ok for me to use the "need" the church had to strike up a conversation with the neighbor. Christ needed water. I needed a plasterer. It seemed a logical stretch and reason enough to initiate a friendly neighborhood chat.

After an initial conversation about the plaster, the Lord began His work. Something was going on in the family that was troubling her. The neighbor was grateful to be able to unburden her concern. Prayer was offered, and she sincerely welcomed it. Christ was present in the prayer and the moment. The next day, this neighbor and her mate showed up at the door of the church. One of the legacy members ran up to greet the visitors, eager to welcome them. He shook their hands. He introduced himself. He welcomed them. And then he immediately gave them what amounted to a "We Used to Be a Cult" video someone had made about us. I honestly cringed. What a way to entice a new couple to want to stay or come back to church! But somehow this couple survived that moment and came back.

It took internal member outreach "follow-up" a while to catch up with successful outreach efforts.

On the one hand, we were faced with the odd continual challenge of evangelizing our existing members, and on the other hand, we continued with our successful community outreach. We made it work.

Chapter 14

CULTS IN COLLISION PART 2: WORKING AGAINST

THE BACKDROP OF AN EX-CULT

DENOMINATION

In the last chapter, I spoke of the tensions that were created by working against an ex-cult backdrop *congregationally*. In this chapter, the focus will be on what it was like for me* to work in such a context *denominationally*.

The early years of "reformation" were amazing. We all stepped into this new phase of ministry as one. But after our initial shared start on this new journey, changes between us began to emerge. It made for sincere conflicts of interest between me and those at our WCG headquarters. We didn't seem as equally yoked together as we could be.

In the first stage of our reformation radical changes were made to give local pastors and churches more autonomy and flexibility. But these changes were rescinded as time went on, as a headquarter-centric denomination still retained (and occasionally flexed the muscle of) a still very hierarchical governmental approach.

The Burden of Working Against an Outdated Hierarchical Polity

For all the incredible bravery it took to defy the wrong doctrinal basis of this once small but far-reaching religious empire, doctrinal reformation did not

---

* I acknowledge at the outset the frailty of my own one-sided point of view here. But this chapter and the next tells this part of my story as it was experienced and understood *by me personally* at this time. And most importantly how it course corrected my focus to go back once again to God's place in my life.

necessarily ensure the governmental transformation of our organization. Good-hearted efforts were made, and initial congregational leeway and freedoms were allowed for, but some twenty-five years after our denominational transformation, some contractions have followed our expansions.

Why?

One thoughtful ex-member who'd spent forty years of her life in the system summarized it this way:

> GCI [WCG] was not only a cult in doctrine but in culture as well. It succeeded in changing its doctrine. But their attempts to change the culture didn't include "how" Headquarters* ran things. Their headquarters did modify their governmental structure to some degree and even created advisory boards, etc. And truly their version was better than Herbert Armstrong's and his cronies' ideas. But the change they effectuated, while perhaps noticeably different to them, was still clouded by their own life experience. Most of these new leaders were second and even third-generation children of the system. They grew up in a cult environment. At the end of the day, their manner of oversight looked different and sounded better, but it was still only a modified version of the ex-cult's hierarchical government they were part of before. And second and third-generation children of the system can still shoehorn new systems that are as controlling and as cultishly hierarchical as before. (Former Grace Communion International member who prefers to be anonymous.)

A man from outside the system who was being recruited to plant a church on the reformed denomination's behalf said it this way:

> "I considered it, but in the end, I simply concluded their governmental system was still too hierarchical and allowed for potential abuse. I told that to the leaders point-blank. They simply stared at me and said nothing. They offered no response." (Anonymous, used with permission.)

---

* The in-house name for the office of the church leadership, historically understood to be truly in charge of the denomination and all its churches.

He added that another leader took him aside afterward and tried to encourage him that it would be different one day, but it wasn't convincing enough to make him want to buy in.

Autonomy Given, Autonomy Contracted

An intentional effort was initially made by our headquarters leadership to not be overbearing and to give local congregations and pastors local autonomy.

But as time went on, perhaps things got too blurry for a headquarters-centric people who were used to members being headquarters-centric. The pendulum swung back and forth from top-down (hierarchical) to bottom-up (congregational) policies, and it was hard to keep up. We were allowed to take up our own offerings at the local level, instead of money being mailed directly to headquarters, but the inflexible fifteen percent "apportionment" that was skimmed off the top was hard for at least some struggling congregations to swallow. At first, we were given the freedom to name our own local churches (hence "CrossRoads"), but later leaders attempted to standardize the way churches looked, even to the point of encouraging them to re-adopt the name of the denomination as their local church name. Denominationally sponsored events became more strongly encouraged and in a passive way required, I began to feel. It seemed like the new leadership was engaged in a bit of recidivism, in their own way, like the church member I wrote about earlier who felt like they "had to go back" to the old way of doing things to find his life footing. Perhaps the thought was that if just maybe we revert to our cultic ways of doing things, with our "culture" being what we held fast to as our distinctive, the continual attrition we were seeing would abate.

Making Disciples "Sonlife" Style – A First Effort at Moving Us Forward

One way we attempted to give ourselves a common language and denomination-wide direction to focus on was to promote the "Sonlife" model of church growth. The "Sonlife" model was a discipling program that keyed off the Great Commission in Matthew 28:18-20. Renaming it the "everyday" commission, the model encouraged churches to make disciples who would make other disciples. More can be learned at Sonlife - Making Disciples the Way Jesus Did.[27]

Many of us, early on, still had a lot of post-reformation zeal in our gut. The Sonlife concept was appealing in that it wasn't just a far-flung Great

Commission we were to engage in. It was more of an everyday commission. Living this out locally and visualizing our neighborhoods as our mission fields were encouraged. This was a top-down initiative from Headquarters that *did* serve local church health.

I was thrilled with this approach, but it didn't sit well with everyone including, and especially, some of my pastoral peers. Surprisingly, this emphasis got quite a bit of kickback. "We're still hurting from our losses," some pastors said. "We need to be comforted at our denominational gathering opportunities, not given more to do." For some, it felt like another form of top-down legalism. A group weary of having to "keep" things didn't want to be given one more thing to do—even the right things. I had difficulty relating to that.

Life Focus Differences Begin to Emerge

Probably inevitably, the divide in WCG between old-school hierarchical and on-the-ground congregational approaches evolved into a divide between the older and younger leaders in the denomination. One young person in our congregation complained to me that there were some in our body who just wanted to be "normal" Christians. They wanted to be like the Christians in mainstream Evangelical Christianity now that they were free to do so. In the Armstrong days, they'd watched a whole world around them longingly with their noses pressed to the glass of Holy Days and Sabbaths. Now they were eager to express their freedom to enter the new world. They were fine with identifying with Christ. But they also wanted to be what "normal" Christians seemed to be to them—more laid back, with church (and even God) having a "tamer" and more manageable place in their lives.

I was offended at the suggestion that my continued passion and hunger for pursuing this zealous life for God's service was too authoritarian or legalistic (or "hardcore" as they called it). I was simply putting in the extra effort I sensed our fellowship needed, and I had high expectations of others. Then again, I thought, maybe I *am* just too intense. In this strange new world of evangelicalism, I was confronted by the irony that making disciples in a cult is in some ways easier because it is top-down. In the short term, fear-motivated disciples are easier to make than grace-motivated ones!

It was clear that my leadership style didn't always mesh with our denomination's theological changes. At my worst, I was still a legalist.* At my best, I constantly resisted the pendulum swing into antinomianism, a cheap grace that leads to false comfort and couch-potato Christianity. And to make matters worse, from at least *some* of our "post-changes" denominational leadership, I started getting a personal "feeling" that we weren't resting *in* Christ as much as we were resting *from* the work he wanted us to join him in.

Emphasis on Retiring

In addition to *resting* in Christ, a growing emphasis was placed on *retiring* in Christ as well. An early emphasis was placed on creating and maintaining a retirement fund out of proceeds that came from selling the organization's pricey properties, built up from years of dedicated headquarters-focused tithing. Part of the proceeds from the sale of a major property holding went to creating a retirement fund. But another part (or so I understood) went toward creating some type of endowment fund to ensure the funding of denominational salaries and office facilities, no matter their ability to inspire growth in our churches. Interestingly, the retirement fund somehow failed in the financial crisis of 2008. It was dissolved, and people on the program received actuarially determined proceeds from it—a very gracious gesture indeed.

But another interesting point, not noticed by many in the field, was that the second fund, the one I thought ensured denominational staffing, somehow did not fail and was left intact. There was no shared decision that included a broad spectrum of the remaining pastors and members as to whether this fund could be used to shore up the failing retirement fund. One long-time respected pastor, near retirement, was devastated about that. We had not yet come out of our cages enough to question financial decisions and details openly and aggressively, and to ask for accountability about things I came to believe should be transparent. We never even asked for listings of salaries and budgets of denominational leaders. Well, most of us didn't. As time went on, and my frustrations increased, I did. I don't think my query endeared me to the headquarters staff. I was told I'd never be given the details I had

---

* Somewhat defensively, I want to say I was also OCD---not just a victim of obsessive control disorder, but of "Orthodox" control disorder!

119

requested. I struggled with thinking my growing frustration with that was just my bad attitude.

Hot Dogs and Safaris and Nehemiah

I remember one time coming home from spending hours at a farmers market selling hot dogs for a fundraiser for our church and using it to meet people and share Christ with them. Even when I wasn't selling hotdogs, I was often at the marketplace. In my biblical naiveté (and I say that tongue in cheek), I still believed the book of Acts taught us all how to work spreading the Kingdom like the apostle Paul. He was often in the marketplace "day by day" (Acts 17:17) reasoning with people, having conversations that counted, and attempting to share the news about Jesus. So was I. I was there every Saturday for a while, and sometimes on weeknights. I was using these opportunities to bring new people to Christ, and eventually, church.

I remember coming home after one such event and my wife telling me about a denominational communication reporting how many of the upper-level leaders in our denomination had gone to Africa to observe our "mission" work there. Several members of the headquarters staff were included in this mission-observation trip. They went to observe our church growth in Africa. Pictures were sent of leaders sitting under tents enjoying the colloquial worship our African "churches" performed. An accompanying call went out that local churches in our worldwide family consider funding the purchase of new tents for these meetings.

But when the touring of the tent meetings was over and touching videos of native African-style worship were uploaded and shared, at least some in the group apparently "recharged" from all this "observing" by going on safari. Facebook posts sharing colorful pictures of this safari began to surface. I don't know how much that trip cost, or who paid for it, or how many went, but less privileged members back home (or at least this one) couldn't help but wonder if the safari fees could have been better purposed to purchase more tents on the spot.

Again, what was going on?

In their defense, look at the cultures these leaders might have been coming from. In our old church, leadership was held at an incredibly high level of esteem and honored deference. In our heyday, our top leader was seen as worthy of receiving a position-honoring salary and of course, the perks that come from international travel. Since he was our version of the High Priest, he was a rightful recipient of such a salary because, after all, the High Priest was given a "tithe of the tithe" (Numbers 18:26). That would equate to one-tenth of all the tithes collected in Israel. These individuals came out of a culture that had given leaders a lot of leeway and respect and, to some degree, entitlement.

For me, what at that time began to look a little like ex-cult entitlement began to wear thin. I was working evenings to meet people and connect them to our ministry; Becky was working forty hours each week, volunteering another 20 with church work, caring for our family, and I was preaching, teaching, evangelizing, giving Bible studies, and selling hot dogs to have an excuse to meet people to possibly bring them to Jesus. It was hard watching at least some personnel be rewarded for all their "hard work" of flying to Africa, enjoying colloquial worship, smiling in photo ops, and then go on a safari.

I couldn't help but notice things like this. Was I being sinfully envious? I even spoke to some people about it. I felt guilty about this because I knew my brothers were just victims of their past and maybe a little too stuck in it. But again, I couldn't stop thinking about the scripture in Nehemiah regarding the effort to rebuild the "broken wall" around Jerusalem after it fell. I saw this as a metaphor for what we were doing with the "fallen" section of the Temple of God that was our denomination:

The next section was repaired by the men of Tekoa, but their nobles would not put their **shoulders** *to the work under their supervisors.* [emphasis mine]
(Nehemiah 3:5)

I know this is a harsh and perhaps unfair critique of our headquarters staff, but it's how some of us felt. And at least I felt comforted that if Nehemiah could make such observations, I was on firm biblical footing for doing so.

In the meantime, I kept on keeping on. These were my brothers. We were all still finding our way. Maybe that was their calling and front-line work was mine. After all, we aren't supposed to compare ourselves to others, right? But I began to envision a disturbing analogy. Our luxurious Titanic of a system built on bad doctrine had been fatally struck by the iceberg of truth. Our churches were indeed deployed as lifeboats to rescue people from drowning in the waters of bad doctrine and a world without an awareness of humanity's inclusion in Christ. But why were the lifeboats still tethered to a sinking headquarters system, keeping that Titanic afloat as well? Did we as an ex-cult ever really cut the cord with the cult?

What were the salaries we were paying? What were the budgets attached to them?

Things just didn't compute.

A Personal Breaking Point—A Disagreement over Using New Patches on Old Wineskins

A personal line-in-the-sand moment occurred for me. It was over a local disagreement that had developed between me and our headquarters about a ministry some of our local young people wanted to lead. It was a great idea and, to a degree, I had encouraged it. But it also included critical new member follow-up care responsibilities. I'd seen many a "John Mark" in our midst often leave or start but not complete ministry assignments when things got hard in their personal lives (Acts 15:37-38). I had worked too hard to make the contacts and generate the growth we were seeing to put the follow-through care of these new congregants in young hands which were inexperienced and still not fully seasoned.

I wasn't against them. I loved these young people dearly. We had opened our home to them, giving them places to stay for key periods of transition in their lives. We had developed with one another true bonds of love in Christ, and I believed they'd always be there for me as I would for them. But to me, it was like Jesus said: you don't put new patches on old wineskins. Young people, like new patches, often contract after normal and natural life issues get in the way. Ease them into more and more responsibility, but don't put on them more than they can bear. "Timothy's" in the church can't be Timothy's without an example-setting Paul to inspire, monitor, mentor, and sometimes correct---and most of all, to lead the way in life-sacrificing passion for the cause of Christ.

Looking back, it's certainly possible that in my own ex-cult baggage I implicitly carried a hierarchal mindset that quashed or "straight-jacketed" the budding enthusiasm of these wonderful young people. I saw some of our new patches, on whom our system had wrongfully relied so heavily to "save" our denomination, begin to contract. In response, I began to "exhort." I can only imagine how these young people saw me. It wasn't easy for them having a Greek Orthodox Protestant pastor in a reforming ex-cult trying to grow a "biblical" and "orthodox" church. These amazing young people may have been new patches, but I as their pastor was stuck between wineskins. We were both products of the cult environment we had been immersed in, bouncing back and forth between the curb of legalism to the curb of antinomianism. For all that we had escaped from being under the influence of Herbert Armstrong, it was so embedded in us we didn't see it; and wounding one another was bound to happen.

Regardless, our headquarters staff and I disagreed at the time on the young leaders' readiness to take on accelerated responsibility. As their pastor and an invested older brother, I felt like I knew what was best for them and for the church. A member of the headquarters staff came to town to emphasize their support for the young people. On one hand, I felt deeply wounded and disrespected. On the other hand, I felt increasing pressure to tend to the issues these young people voiced so they would stay in the denomination. My own personal insecurities and fears that I had mismanaged their concerns contributed to the stress.

All of this prompted me to stay close to my flock when I should have been by my ailing mother's bedside. To this day I regret that I did not get more time with Mom while she was on her deathbed. I realize that many people get much less than seven days with a dying parent. But this loss magnified the loss of leaving them twenty-six years before in the city I'd grown up in to "find my brothers," only now to realize that my brothers were turning against me.

In the weeks after Mom's death, it felt like I had little space to grieve. I continued to be warned that if I didn't tend well to our young people, and heed their voices, our future leaders might leave the church. I know it's a perspective full of feelings and susceptible to bitterness, but it felt like my superiors in GCI cared more about keeping the young people and not as much about shepherding me as I was processing the magnitude of my mother's loss. We older guys needed to fade away. It was these young people they wanted.

It was heartbreaking. Our children stopped attending church with us. They no longer wanted anything to do with the denomination after that. They knew some of the local dynamics at play and were appalled that our leaders had not backed up their dad. I had left my mother and father, my culture, my original church, and a lifetime I could have shared living locally with them as they

123

aged and lived out their Golden Years. My mother's death underscored the lost years of life I could have shared with her but for helping this church rebuild and take care of its people as Dad told me to do. Yes, it was a very different church than the one I left to follow Herbert Armstrong in WCG, but GCI's church leaders were the same men I had gone through Ambassador with and with whom I had logged decades of Christian service.

I was deeply offended. And they were upset with *me*. A distancing developed between myself and our denominational leadership that solidified my growing sense of detachment and alienation.

Pastoring a Very Protesting Protestant Herd of Cats

It was a strange amalgam of people we'd drawn to our WCG/GCI church during those "pinnacle years" at CrossRoads. Some of them were newer church attenders whose fairly recent form of group community experience was Alcoholics Anonymous. Some of them were Baby Boomers who had checked out of involvement with Christ and church years ago. Others were young people in crisis, or young people just searching for something more. Some were long-time members from traditional churches that were run more congregationally in nature, and probably more in keeping with the good old-fashioned "let's give everybody/everything a voice" American way. We even had one Christian who had migrated to Judaism and then came back to Christianity. Of course, we had newly liberated "ex-cult" members still with us as well. Some were still in their cages of old practices with doors open but too scared to come out. Some were hungry to assert (probably over-assert) their power to choose what had been denied them at the zenith of their cult's hierarchical days.

The denominational heartaches I mentioned above were not enough to quench the overriding sense of congregational passion and joy we were experiencing in Christ. Emerging from the WCG world, we did not have the same awareness of Jesus Christ that Christendom had known about for 2,000 years. We had discovered him, recovered preaching him, and were in love with him. For a while, even this herd of cats we were pastoring (ex-cult members, along with new members) were having an amazing time discovering that same Jesus together. I was playing my spiritual heart out. The Jesus of John community-connection ministry was bearing significant fruit. The Lord was at work in us and in our town and the joy was contagious.

At our Christmas service in 2014, fifteen years into our walking and calling ministry, we managed to squeeze 250 people into the building. It only seemed appropriate that we would perform a baptism requested by a mother that night. As a standing-room-only crowd gathered around the beloved child, all the adversity of recent years seemed to melt away. Things could not have been better. But the big storm was coming.

Chapter 15

THE LEFT HAND OF FELLOWSHIP

A little over two years after that unforgettable Christmas service, Becky and I found ourselves on the way to a Panera Bread location near our home, where we were joining two denominational officials for a special meeting with us they had arranged.

We had left our families to serve in this church. We had sacrificed and worked passionately for this our entire adult lives. It was a ministry in which we felt we had found, at least for a while, a true spiritual community. In this church, we felt we'd finally found a people who would follow the Bible faithfully, including loving people and staying loyal to them as the Bible dictated. In them, we felt we had found "forever brothers" in Christ.

Emerging from WCG, we in GCI proclaimed that we had been "transformed by the truth." Indeed, we had made great headway, at least doctrinally. By the decree of the National Association of Evangelicals, we were no longer a cult.

But that night at Panera felt like a step back in time.

That night, at a table by the public restrooms, Becky and I were read a letter notifying us that we were both being removed from the church where we'd served as pastors for nearly 28 years. There had been complaints, we were told. Just what these complaints were, we were not made privy too, for reasons of "confidentiality." We were not allowed to know what the complaints were, who the complainers were, or to even be given a chance to respond. We were just being let go.

Wait. We were being let go?

I can't tell you how both stunned and numbed we were when we first heard that.

We were being let go by the denomination that we had sojourned with for forty years since our college graduation from its Bible College in Big Sandy, Texas. A severance check for almost $30,000 was being offered to us. "We don't normally do this," said one of the representatives tersely, almost dismissively. But I guess unworthy though we were, it was being offered anyway. And there were strings attached. We would have to sign what I assume was an NDA (Non-Disclosure Agreement) that to me seemed full of "promise not to sue" clauses. We had to agree to not communicate with any of our church members (via phone, in person, or text) for a specified period as a condition for receiving this "one-time" offer. The offer, by the way, was good only until the next morning at 11 a.m. We might, we were told, be "allowed" to come back to the church God used us to replant and grow. But that would be only after six months. And it was to be only at "the discretion" of the regional pastor. Truly, we thought, this wasn't happening. Without even consulting each other, Becky and I refused the money.

I had no warning this was coming. Even as recently as six months earlier, my record had been praised for our baptisms by a denominational representative. I was even told I might be selected for some special new ministry training coming down the pike.

I have already alluded to those who thought my leadership style was too confining and to the young people who thought I was "hardcore" and felt like my emphasis on the commands of Christ was at odds with a grace-based lifestyle. Looking back at that time, I can see some merit in a recognition that my style as a pastor with that group may not have always couched the biblical imperatives in the indicatives of grace in a way they especially needed after being raised in a very hierarchical system.

If being raised in two authoritarian environments (Greek Orthodox and WCG) wasn't enough, it never dawned on me at the time that the bullying abuse I suffered as a boy had the post-traumatic potential to cause me to stiffen my resolve against allowing myself to be disrespected in the same way again---with the potential, I see now, of at least sometimes coming across as too authoritarian and "abrasive" myself.

So, I wasn't everyone's best friend either in the denomination or at CrossRoads. But there were many, many people who loved us, loved our ministry, and saw Christ's service in our lives. There were so many we brought to Christ and a deeper understanding of Scripture than they'd ever experienced. And any criticism I felt from within was more than mitigated by the affirmation I received from the denomination for leading a transformational church, one to be emulated to the point of being featured in a denominational documentary film. (After almost a whole week of filming by a camera crew of three who had been flown in from the West Coast, the project was mysteriously dropped.)

How did we get here? What did I specifically do wrong that precipitated this drastic measure? I remember the day a concerned church member told me that someone had told him that our local "church leadership" was being investigated. The regional representative over us flatly denied it. "I would never do that," he told me and my wife. "Not without talking with you first." But that's not how things played out.

The GCI administration manual had been written early in the years of the denomination's reformation when their passion to not emulate abusive hierarchical control was still fresh. It had assured that pastors would be kept in the loop if ever serious allegations were made about them. But this group of leaders felt no such obligation to adhere to their stated policy at this time. They were ready for my severance from the organization, or so it seemed. A decision was made without our involvement in any due process. They also mistakenly failed to involve a significant and much larger portion of our congregation's input than just those of the complainers. That would come back to haunt them embarrassingly one night later. But for us that night at Panera, there was to be no dialogue or brotherly discussion. We were simply cast out.

Why again were we fired? What stood out most to me in a communication our lawyer received from them in writing a few weeks later, was this: We are "a hierarchical religious organization." In short, they were reinforcing their right by law to terminate me without reason or cause or notice.* And that was it. No apology was offered, no clarifications were given. A friend later told us they were told we were not being let go for any "moral or ethical" reasons. And my wife remembers that we were told our termination had nothing to do with "moral or financial" reasons. But the local "sensational drama"

---

* See https://www.churchlawandtax.com/library/pastor-church-law/chapter-8/termination-of-employees/.

created by the situation implicitly encouraged people to fill the vacuum with rumors and false allegations.*

"Are these people even Christian?" asked a neighbor next to the church. She knew me and knew particularly how I served both the community and her family. She couldn't understand. And I couldn't explain. Were we dealing with a group of Christian brothers, zealous for truth and reconciliation? Or were we dealing with a savvy ex-cult's legal system, which still knew how to protect itself as it had to do so many times before in its cult days?

It was hard to tell.

What Happened Next

Not knowing what else to do, Becky and I walked out of the meeting as quickly as we could. One of the denominational leaders hastened to add as we were walking out: "Remember, this money is only available until tomorrow morning." To me, he had a concerned look on his face. And I didn't get the sense the concern was about us. I don't think he or they ever dreamed we would reject the money and the "gag order" that went with it. I think it began to make them afraid of what might result if word about all this got out.

Again, not knowing what to do, we drove up to our church building's fellowship hall where I had spent so many late nights for two decades. A new church member was there leading an outreach discipleship class. She and those working with her (her husband and another couple, both dear friends) knew the members who had stopped attending and were probably some of the sources of the complaints. They also were familiar with the dynamics involved and the attitudes behind them. Our friends were anxious to know what had happened at our meeting with the denominational representatives. We had told them we would let them know as soon as possible.

We quietly went to the building, careful not to interrupt the class, and gave them an update privately. None of us spoke to anybody else attending the class, by the way. We came in unobtrusively. Someone besides one of our

---

* Even when it got to the point that some clearly false allegations had been made against us that were beginning to spread through the community, we discovered we were not even entitled to an apology. Any wrong that they admitted, any apology or even clarification, I assume could legally upend their decision, so we were left to be vilified.

four friends was leading the class at this point, so we quietly got the attention of our four friends and had them join us in the kitchen. We reported what had transpired. All of us stood together in the kitchen of the meeting hall, all of us in shock, and all of us trying to figure out what had just happened.

Then the next wave of disaster hit.

A Badly Misdirected Mass Email

The ones who fired us must have been very fearful that we'd somehow contact the whole congregation before they could. We had no intention of doing so. But apparently, they sent out a hastily written email to the congregational listserv, which included the room full of members engaged in the class. It said something to the effect that Pastor Jim was no longer pastor of the church, and implied that I was not to be heeded as such. This was all happening in real-time, and people began to read the news on their phones.

These people were leaning into what we were teaching at CrossRoads, growing in their faith. They knew us, loved us, and trusted us. To the fiber of their beings, they all felt this was wrong. Like us, they were now totally and completely shocked. A young teen was crying. People were astir. They didn't understand. Becky and I still chose not to speak to any of them. We were frankly too stunned to do anything but remain in the company of the two couples in the kitchen with us and try to wrap our minds around this. But the lady in charge of the class felt she had her hand forced by the email that had come out. People were upset and asking questions. She felt she had to explain. When she did, people just got more and more agitated.

But that wasn't the worst of it.

Those at church that night were not the only ones who had received the email. *My Greek family back home in Alabama was on the list!* I'd broken their hearts forty years ago when I left their beloved Greek Orthodox Church to serve God in another system. So were members of the community I had included on this email list that I thought might want to be "updated about our activities." We'd become quite a "community" church, and I had become a well-known and visible community figure. They got these emails too.

My family knew I'd stayed with this group to help them after their doctrinal reformation instead of leaving them as so many did. They were also proud that so much of our ministry had been blessed with acknowledged success. They were shocked and alarmed. The cult I'd left them for was kicking their brother out. Community members who held me in a position of trust and respect received communication that shamed us publicly for no reason.

Information control mechanisms can be swift and brutal. I'd never experienced anything like this directed towards me until then, but I can assure you——they are swift and brutal. It was heartbreaking.

And it was going to get worse.

Our Last Moments in the Building

With our heads spinning, we made our way to the parking lot, trying to keep out of the crowd, trying to figure out what to do next. People came up to console us, comfort us, and reassure us. So, finally, we did speak to them. We just thanked them and encouraged them to have faith in God. He would take care of things. It only seemed right to do this.

My wife had texted our daughters, and the one who lived nearest came to the church to be with us. She had to practically hold our hands, guiding us to take a few action steps, like picking up any personal possessions we might want to take with us. There was a poster of my granddaughter I'd painted and used as a logo for our church outreach café. I decided to take it with me.

And there was a clear acrylic "globe" being held by a clear acrylic hand that looked like God "holding the world" in His hand. I'd bought it at a used goods sale for $5 with personal funds to be used for ministry. I took that too. Those were the only two things we took. I didn't even think about the desk they'd given me a few years ago for Pastor Appreciation month. I didn't think about much of anything, except for the fact that I couldn't believe this was happening.

What Do We Do Now?

The members eventually went home. Becky and I were left alone in the empty building with the two couples we talked with about the firing. One of them mentioned thoughtfully, "We might all want to take our own personal possessions out of the building. I've been in similar situations like this. They're liable to change the locks." One of them, a worship leader, had many personal items of sound and amplification equipment he had loaned to the church. He thought it best to take them back home. The Sunday School director (also the lady in charge of the class that night) was using a lot of her resources for the classes she was teaching. She gathered those together as well. They took their personal items, and my wife and I walked away with our plastic globe and the picture of our granddaughter.

We drove home in shock and disbelief that nearly forty years of loyal and sacrificial involvement in this organization had ended this way. For years, we'd been held up as an example for renewing and replanting churches.

What were we going to do? The week was going to become still more surreal.

The Meeting with the Church the Following Night

We'd been asked to arrange a follow-up meeting for the denominational representatives with the church's leadership the night following our meeting with them. We dutifully obliged, like trusting lambs being led to the slaughter, not knowing it would be their effort to share with the leadership their rationale for letting us go, and perhaps win them over to their point of view. To their surprise—and ours—virtually the whole church showed up at this meeting. Word had spread to the congregation, and they wanted answers, too.

I personally talked with only one other active member the following day, a dear friend I baptized and brought to Christ, whose love I valued and still value today. She said she was going to the meeting to hear what was going on and to decide what was happening for herself. I encouraged her to do so. I encouraged her to go and to listen to whatever "they" had to say, even though we wouldn't be there to defend ourselves from any one-sided allegations. I encouraged her to listen and make up her own mind. It seemed morally and ethically honorable to not try to influence her decision. We were going to leave this in God's hands.

Someone tried to encourage us to attend that meeting, but another friend wisely counseled us not to go. Let whatever happens happen, he advised. Don't be a part of influencing it in any way.

So that night, Becky and I took a nervous walk through our neighborhood, agonizingly waiting while this fateful meeting transpired. Members listened to what the two representatives from our denominational headquarters had to say. Apparently, what they had to say, and how they said it, didn't win many of them over. Even how they came across was received negatively.

To be truthful, these church members had not had much exposure to our denominational leadership face-to-face. I had had concerns about how they would come across considering the passionate and hardworking Christianity I tried to model and preach. Some had come in for an official church visit not too long before and, to some, they'd come across negatively. Their tendency to speak in the context of the "inside culture" they still primarily functioned in didn't translate well. This group had some strong things to say about what they were confronted with that night.

"They didn't even start in prayer until I asked them," one member reported. "I had to remind them to do so." They were used to me always starting everything off with prayer.

From that point forward the meeting did not go well for the denominational representatives. When one of them denied saying something six people heard him say three months earlier, they'd had enough. One man stood up, put his keys to the building on the table, and walked out the door. Another large group rose, put their keys on the table, and did the same. The room was soon emptied, with just a few members (most of them long-time members of the old church), left in the room.

This was no longer about what Pastor Jim and Becky had done. This was about the majority of the congregation rejecting both the representatives and the group they represented. These denominational representatives to me had always seemed less experienced in dealing with mindsets that were not part of their self-contained, in-house denominational culture. The local members immediately reacted with both distrust of them and the group they represented. Their words didn't justify firing a couple these folks had grown to love for what they shared with them in Christ.

They were not going to be part of that package. They didn't yet know how, but they were going to express their faith in other ways, and they still wanted me and my wife in their lives.

Being "Marked," Romans 16:17 Style? *

The *coup de grâce* would come the following day—the day after the disastrous meeting with the members. I received a phone call from a GCI elder in another state. He was someone I didn't know, but who had concerns, actually some indignation, about the "cultish" nature he still saw in our system. He

---

* Romans 16:17-18 (KJV): 17 Now I beseech you, brethren, mark them which
cause divisions and offences contrary to the doctrine which ye have learned; and avoid them.

warned me, in a kind but serious voice, that an extremely hurtful email was being sent around the denomination about me. I *thought* it implied something to the effect that I was divisive, and in our former Worldwide Church of God/Grace Communion International world, perhaps accompanied by a warning about anything "divisive" I might share. Memories of individuals being "marked" in the old "cult" days of the church came to mind. Once you were marked (like being banned or shunned in the Amish community) you became cut off from the body of Christ as the denomination presumed itself to be. I never saw the letter so I can't directly comment on it. He tried to prepare me so I wouldn't be devastated. I honestly don't remember his name, but his kindness and concern were real.

Something along those lines must have at least been perceived by some. A young lady, who was a non-member but associated with an outreach Bible study I led for a member of her community, was very upset about my firing. I had brought her grandfather to Christ and baptized him just before he died of cancer the year before. She asked, "Why aren't we allowed to talk to you?" Was I marked? When you were marked in the old system, people were not allowed to talk to you. Is that what some understood? Why was she told she shouldn't or perhaps *couldn't* talk with me?

My wife Becky had already been registered for a GCI-associated ministry training seminar when the pastor leading it told her she could no longer be involved. He added she might be able to later "once Jim's good name was restored."

What had been said to tarnish it? To whom had it been said? Another in this denomination, a lady eager for my wife to continue in her parachurch ministry, admitted, "Our church has hurt a lot of people." When my wife queried, she said she had seen some email about us but couldn't find it anymore. Was it as hastily removed as it had been written? I wonder what might have surfaced if we had taken legal action and it involved "discovery."

Again, having been conditioned by cult in-house behavior rules for years, I blamed myself for this email having been written. Surely, I made this happen because of what I said. Many abused wives blame themselves for the abuse they receive. Perhaps being in a cult conditions one to smear oneself with that type of blame-taking too. I have no idea the extent that the hierarchical cultish control I was under has affected my psyche, causing self-disparagement, not to mention the ways it may have caused me as a victim to repeat the same errors of my abusers, personal or systemic.

The Final Communication—In Writing

I took no ownership for the letter we did see that came out two days later. It came to us from the denomination's legal department. It contained even more hurtful statements. It came with more papers for us to sign. And it came with clearly untrue allegations.

I was accused of "disrupting meetings" (plural). I never did. I was accused of "removing essential church equipment." (I never did). I was presented with an offer of a much lower amount of money since I was disruptive and perhaps by now even publicly perceived as an "essential equipment looting" thief. Again, it contained "I agree not to sue clauses" that were highlighted to make sure they were seen and signed. I ignored it. I knew also, and sadly, I had to seek out the help of a lawyer to know what to do next.

Never did I dream the Sunday before that I'd be giving my last sermon as pastor in our church building. Never did I dream I'd be facing this week of cult-like hell from the people I had served so passionately for so many years.

As a Greek Orthodox, I'd been a Christian in a culture cult.

As a passionate member and pastor in WCG, I'd been a Christian in a doctrinal and hierarchical cult.

As an Evangelical in GCI, I'd been a Christian in a still struggling and reforming ex-cult.

For now, I was none of these.

Because despite all that had just happened, I was still a Christian in Christ.

And God was still there!

Chapter 16

GOD WAS STILL THERE

It was the kids at the playground all over again. My new peers on my spiritual playground who had been our spiritual family for years---those with whom I had shared the joys of our unique, one-of-a-kind, doctrinal reformation---these brothers surrounded me and questioned the very core of my being. They, too, didn't want to play with me anymore and cast me out.

I know how Joseph felt. I know how Hagar felt too. I also began to wonder how Esau felt because, to see it from both sides, I began to wonder (or fear) I was more like him than like Joseph and Hagar. Maybe I was worthy of being cast out. I wracked my brain biblically to figure out who I was in this story. I honestly didn't know, and I know I was not entirely without fault. Maybe in some ways, I was a little bit of all of them? But I continued to scour biblical examples to see which ones applied in this situation.

A whole life journey, a whole life's work, went up in smoke. Even agnostic friends and non-attending family of church members were astonished. "What the hell?" was said more than once by those who heard.

It was hard not to feel that the people letting us go did not have the emotional sensitivity, the spiritual compassion, or simply even the desire to reach out to me and hear my story. They didn't want to listen to where I was coming from or to discuss my intentions. A mechanistic succession program, based on age, availability, and perceived loyalty to the culture of the system does not necessarily produce sensitive and compassionate leadership. Perhaps I assumed, the decision-makers were still too new in their "freedom" in Christ to recognize what they were doing to us personally, and how hurtful it was to us. Maybe they didn't realize all the nuances of what they were doing. Or maybe they didn't care or think they had to care.

I had long noticed the cultural shift in GCI after "the changes." We were all still finding our way. When the confines of cultic rule were thrown off, the pendulum swung wildly away from legalism. People seemed to find permission to be free to express all kinds of latent and repressed behaviors in the name of freedom. Maybe I was not as "freed-up" as I should have been, and to the decision-makers too critical and autocratic. Perhaps in the name of Christian liberty, they felt free to be what seemed to us so hard-lined, so hurtful. But this episode seemed to me so much like the cult we had been in the past. Again, perhaps it was a perfect storm of ex-cult trauma on both sides manifesting in different ways.

What was worse was the immediate shutdown of practically all relationships with our peers because of the warnings about me our friends received. This is a small but noticeable example: we immediately noticed a precipitous drop in the "likes" we received on our Facebook posts, save from a very few friends who perhaps, in their own way, wanted to show support.

How many of us have washed our hands and looked the other way when an organization we were a part of caused harm to someone else in the organization? To us, many of our local friends in the system did exactly what we did when things like this happened to others in the past: they looked the other way. Regarding our local church, people we had brought to Christ, and people who only knew each other because of the work Christ had done through us, looked the other way, giving the organization the benefit of the doubt. For Becky and me, the compounding levels of betrayal crushed our souls.

I entered a dark night full of self-incrimination and self-doubt. I was so disoriented I barely knew who I was in life, much less who I was in the Scripture. Despite all that happened, however, by the grace of God I can say with gratitude:

God was still there.

God was still there.

God was still there!

He was there in love, in warmth, and even in emotional support. Nothing happened that dissuaded me from believing this whole journey was still all about God. And *God was still there!*

When I left my family and my much beloved Greek Orthodox culture in which my total sense of self-identity had been wrapped, I came to God, not a cult. I had sensed God's call, and some of my Greek brethren thought I'd left them, God's one true church, and their cherished culture behind—but *God was still there!* He was guiding me, blessing me, leading me all the way, despite my doctrinal misunderstanding.

When the "cult" bravely repented and reformed its doctrines, *God was still there!* He was blessing us, comforting us, giving us new visions of hope, and leading us into greater truths about Jesus.

When God used us to transform the legacy members of the local congregation to orthodox Christianity and Christian practices, *God was still there!* He was smiling at us, loving us, and giving us moments of great achievement and satisfaction.

When he taught us how to become a thriving community church respected by many leaders in Tipp City, and when we pinnacled with standing room only at our Christmas service, *God was still there!* He had miraculously amassed a hodgepodge of new members from all kinds of backgrounds, some with and some without previous faith journeys.

When members within the church became concerned with the behaviors of some of our younger, not yet seasoned-by-life leaders, *God was still there!* He was leading us, strengthening us, and even giving us new members despite the adversity. Newer people with different attitudes were added to our number, helping us to rebuild and flourish despite the expansions and contractions I'd come to believe would always occur in a Christ-like Christian ministry, and that I'd frankly learned to simply ride out.

In spite of our struggles with "corporate" in recent years, we had re-committed our hearts to the denomination, choosing to submit to the leadership of individuals we'd been scared to trust. When that leadership fired us and offered us a severance with what seemed to be cult-like strings attached, God was still there! He gave us the courage to refuse the money.[*]

---

[*] An interesting corollary to this is that in the next year, for reasons still inexplicable to this day, money in our checking account mysteriously increased. We found ourselves with more savings than we ever had. My wife could not account for where the money came from. But when it came to our financial needs, like Elisha's widow's oil and wheat jars that never emptied, God was still there.

We began this journey not for the money but for God and with God. We knew that, and so did He.

We did not become bitter. We were confused. We were discouraged. We were crushed. We were publicly shamed and humiliated. Unchecked narratives led others to believe that we and our supporters "stole" things from the church before we "left" and "split the church," taking members with us. But through it all *God was still there!* And he manifested our next steps in some amazing ways.

God Was Still There – In My Big Fat Northern and Southern Greek Family

As soon as Becky and I told our daughters and word got around, telephone calls of love, compassion, and support immediately poured in. One son-in-law canceled a scheduled family trip to his family in another state. Others communicated actions and messages of support. God was still there in my immediate family and the love we shared.

Especially meaningful, God was still there in my family of origin. All my siblings registered shock and dismay at what had happened and were on our side, whatever that side was. And all my siblings, broken-hearted though they were when I left the Greek Orthodox Church, still expressed love and concern for me and not "I told you so." God was still there, in my immediate and extended family.

God was still there in my friends, too, with the people who stood up for me at the meeting with the denominational leaders the night following my firing. I will forever be grateful to them. They are dear brothers and sisters in Christ and are still a part of my heart and life.

There were others as well. One dear brother whose theology I deeply respect and one of the few in leadership whose spirituality I resonated with, had stepped down from his role in the denomination and its leadership the very same month I was fired. God *was* and still *is* there in that friend. A good friend from our college days just happened to call that week, for the first time in decades. He, like me, was no longer in our system. He, like me, came into the church as a Christian. He, like me, was a Christian in a cult. He just felt moved to call me, he said. And he called to remind me that it was forty years to the day when we graduated as roommates and close friends from our church's

Ambassador College. It was easy to see the number 40 in all kinds of biblical ways after that phone call. Maybe there was some merit to it?

Ever so dimly, I was beginning to see that we're not supposed to be Christians acting out of our cults. We're supposed to be Christians living out of our collective oneness in Christ. And it's not just Christians that are *in* Christ. My Greek "culture" cult eyes had not allowed me to see it. My doctrinal "cult" cult eyes had kept me blinded from it. And my last "culture" cult, that of American Evangelicalism, might have been the most effective in keeping all of us in the dark.

Now the scales have fallen off and I can see:

All humanity is in Christ!

Done with any version of "us vs them" Christianity, by God's grace I was ready for my new theologically grounded expression.

Chapter 17

CULTS IN COLLISION PART 3: TRINITARIAN CHRISTIANITY VS AMERICAN SENSE OF SELF

My experience of American Evangelicalism was like a nested box inside of my WCG/GCI journey. In other words, my experience in my third cultic expression actually occurred within the general organizational structure of the second. As I've discussed, some things stayed relatively the same, even if the name was eventually changed. When WCG moved from "the fringe to the fold" in the mid-90s and was welcomed by the Evangelical Churches of America, I as a WCG (and eventually GCI) pastor entered the steep learning curve of not only mainstream, "doctrinally correct" Christianity, but of Evangelicalism---and I wasn't sophisticated enough to appreciate the nuances and distinctions of this popularly accepted "flavor" of the faith.

There was some irony in our shift into the fold of Evangelicalism, because the one who had led us out of Armstrong's doctrine, President Joseph Tkach, Sr. was at the time under the guiding influence of those who would not consider themselves Evangelicals at all! One of the things that Joseph Tkach, Sr. emphasized in his long message about "the changes" was the fact that God was Trinity. Under the leadership of Tkach (himself influenced by Greek scholar Kyriakos Stavrinides) and through scholar John McKenna (of the T.F. Torrance school), we were all introduced to a way of thinking about the Trinity that is often underappreciated by Evangelicals. That this strain of nontypical Trinitarian thinking existed in GCI from its inception into Evangelicalism cannot be overlooked.*

In fact, I would say one of the more positive theological distinctives of GCI was the way we eventually welcomed Trinitarian thinkers especially influenced by James and T.F. Torrance, scholars like C. Baxter Kruger, Gary Deddo, and Jeff McSwain. The video series "You're Included" featured these and many teachers of the same ilk, and the videos and publications are still circulating on YouTube and in printed form. Ironically, in a sense these teachings chaffed against our new confines in the ECA, and this is something that GCI has continued to deal with.

In a weird way, even while I was with GCI, this kind of Trinitarian teaching that we received after "the changes" connected the dots back to my Greek Orthodox roots and prepared me for the next stage of my ministry career. In fact, I can't help but think now in hindsight that perhaps my having been "simmered" in Trinitarian love in the Greek Orthodox church is what saved me from the more crippling aspects of legalism in WCG and the rugged individualism of Evangelicalism that came after (what the Torrances would call semi-Pelagianism).

It took me a while for these dots to emerge with clarity. In the meantime, I stood firm to my call as a pastor, even after GCI fired me and we (by "we" I mean all the folks from CrossRoads who still wanted me as their pastor) planted a new church across town.** But throughout my tenure with CrossRoads until now, the Trinity has been more and more prominent in my thinking. This has looked like:

- A greater emphasis on the "personhood" of humanity—the human *person* (located in the unity and mutual love of Trinitarian *Persons*) as opposed to the American rugged individualist thinking.

---

* For what it's worth, the wife of Tkach, Sr. came from a Greek family and Greek Orthodox background. In some sense both of them had exposure to an "Orthodox" culture steeped from its inception in what I can only describe as a Trinitarian inspired sense of communion and belonging. Perhaps that's why the most repeated slogan of his tenure of service was "We Are Family."

** To be clear, two leaders from the former CrossRoads leadership team planted this church. They invited me to serve as their pastor at this plant. But I did not, as some have thought, plant this church. I did gratefully respond to their invitation to serve as its pastor, immediately. The church (Community Connexions Church) is still in existence today, and one of its founders is now serving as its pastor.

- An understanding of inclusion that is narrowly defined by Jesus Christ—true God and true human—and who he is as the Second Adam in whom all human beings are included.
- Resultingly, a more egalitarian and less hierarchical ecclesial model.

Understanding of The Trinity and the Spirit of Connection

When I finally began to understand that the New Covenant was all about Christ, the 2,000 years of Christian thought processing began to make sense. I can see now why the early church became transfixed with the unfolding revelation that God was a Trinity. I can understand and identify with their healthy obsession with the Trinity in those early years. I became obsessed with it, too.

Especially intriguing to us was the fact that (whether you use the pronoun he or she) the Holy Spirit wasn't an "it." We had spent so many years minimizing the Spirit as merely the power of God. We did not see "it" as a Person communing with the other Trinitarian Persons, and we, therefore, underappreciated the Spirit's role in our lives with Christ, lifting us up to "live into" our identity as beloved children of God (Romans 8:15). It's taken me years to just begin to see how critical this understanding is. And its truths are still unfolding.

After his resurrection, Jesus ascended to heaven as a human being. Having received the Holy Spirit on all humanity's behalf, he subsequently poured it out on "all" flesh (Acts 2:33). The Spirit of God, we might say, has given us "Free God Wi-Fi." All have access to it because we're already "in it" by living and moving and having our being "in" Christ (Acts 17:28).

Since this Spirit of connection is purposely at work everywhere, the way to connect with non-believers is not to hit them over the head with a Bible and its rules. It's not to default to the American way of "rugged individualism" which tells us that we don't belong to God unless *we* do something, unless *we* completely yield to God, unless *we* make Christ the center of our lives, until *we* get baptized, walk the aisle, or say the sinner's prayer, etc. That is the audacity of individualism, not the economy of the gospel. The good news is not about what *we* have done for God (or not done!) but about what God has done for us as our Creator and Redeemer.

Instead of a measly invitation for us as "individuals" to respond or give "our" consent to the "almighty" Individual in heaven (God), to preach Jesus Christ is a bold proclamation of the blessings and accountability of *already and always having belonged* to God. Jesus had told the soon-to-be apostle Paul "it hurts you, Saul, to kick against the goads!" (Acts 26:14). In other words, it's hard to go against the grain of the primal Life in whose being you live, Saul. It's like kicking against sharp goads, or getting splinters when you run your hand against a grain of wood. It simply doesn't work.

No, the gospel is so much better than that! It's about going out to the people and telling them they *already have a place in Christ, in God*. It's about opening their eyes to Christ and the Spirit sent by the Son and the Father. It's about helping them to discover where the Triune God is already at work in their lives. It's about developing an awareness of Christ's "faith-full (full of faith) presence" already in their lives. In sum, it's about helping our brothers and sisters to see where Jesus exists in their lives *as the deepest reality*, in the midst of all the hurt and pain, and in constant *healing care* and love. God is not randomly here or there, He is a constant presence in our lives, and *at work on purpose*.*

When you approach God's love and presence in all people in this way, the possibilities for discovering Kingdom manifestations become endless. Since free God Wi-Fi has indeed fallen on all flesh, that means God's Spirit is meeting you in the people you cross paths with every day, in every child, every teacher, every worker, every server, every medical professional, every checkout cashier, in every marketplace, every gym, every retail store, every hair salon, every *everything*. "Where can I go from your Spirit? Where can I flee from your presence?" the Psalmist declares (Psalm 139:7). Such a perspective fills our lives with adventure and expectation. It's complex, but we are called to discern this dimension of God's presence even in our enemies.

As Jesus shared with his disciples just before his death (John 15:18-27), if unbelievers oppose you, or if unbelievers accept your teaching, they don't necessarily know who they are opposing or who they are obeying. Our job, Jesus continues, is to testify about *him*, to prayerfully endeavor to move people from *concepts* to a personal knowledge of *him*---Christ---and of his

---

* The italicized phrases above, *the deepest reality*, *at work on purpose* and *healing care* point specifically to three ministry expressions that I think have tapped into the Trinitarian life of God for the benefit of many. More to say about that later.

already present "Presence" in our lives. "This is eternal life," Jesus said, "that they might know you, the only true God, and Jesus Christ whom you have sent" (John 17:3). Even if they're not calling Him the right name yet, it doesn't matter. Just like the good folks at Alcoholics Anonymous discovered, God will even accept the name Higher Power or The Universe. Did you reject your babies when they couldn't say Dada or Mama yet? I think you get the point.

Regardless of whether or not we feel "full of the Spirit," * we can help facilitate others' awareness of the ever-present Spirit by our faithful presence with them, and our willingness to take a little time to get to know them, getting under the surface of the mundane. What a joy to point out the good fruit of the Spirit in them so that they might see Who it is that is empowering the good they are doing!

How It's Beginning to Play Out

I had already started a fledgling outreach ministry based on this approach at my former church CrossRoads before I was separated from GCI (euphemism for "they fired me"). I created a 501(c)3 called CrossRoads ConneXions. It was a faith-inspired, but not faith-imposing, nonprofit, a vehicle of outreach to connect people from all walks of life through the Spirit of ConneXion. I chose to spell the word with the upper case "X" rather than the "ct." The "X" was my way of including the cross of Christ, the one who connects us all.

The reason behind the name is simple. Christ is the CrossRoads, the intersection where God and humanity come together in the God-Human, and because of this union, the Spirit of ConneXion is now available and active everywhere. I felt inspired to give it this motto: "connecting real needs, good deeds, and people from all walks of life." If any good is being done anywhere in this world, it's being done by the Spirit of ConneXion anyway. Why not let them know how they have already been accepted and included in the life of Christ?

---

* I like to use the phrase "Holy Spirit hot spot" for that---but that is in no way to imply that some of us are "hotter" than others. To be "full of the Spirit" is a biblical expression regarding the manifestation of the fullness of Spirit that Christ has given every person in himself- "you have been given fullness in Christ" (Col 2:10). It's not like a container that is either full of water or not, as if some people have more of the Spirit than others. Instead, to be "full of the Spirit" is this fullness experienced in palpable, visceral, and transformational ways at some times more than others.

At CrossRoads, I attempted to open the church for all kinds of what I called ConneXion activities: food banks, pay-it-forward cafes, clothing giveaways, etc. But it never really took off. One reason was because it was in a church, and I stepped on a few toes when the fellowship hall was filled with items to be given away to those in need and looked like a perpetual garage sale. I couldn't sell the vision well enough to win over the possessors of those toes.

It had taken me forty years, but the time of wandering was done. It was time to do ministry in a new way—by the Spirit of ConneXion. It was time to step out of the often toxic and relatively ineffective version of local church ministry I'd been in. It was time to step into the Promised Land, the Kingdom of Heaven, which is near. It was time to do so with the Spirit of ConneXion who has indeed fallen on *all* flesh. All means *all*, as the verses below proclaim (emphasis mine throughout).

> *One died for **all**, and therefore **all** died.* (2 Corinthians 5:14)

> *And I, when I am lifted up from the earth,* I will draw **all** people to myself.* (John 12:32)

> *For **all** have sinned and fall short of the glory of God, and **all** are justified freely through the redemption that came by Christ Jesus.* (Romans 3:23-24)

> *Consequently, just as one trespass resulted in condemnation for **all** people, so also one righteous act resulted in justification and life for **all** people.* (Romans 5:18)

> *For God was pleased to have **all** his fullness dwell in him, and through him to reconcile to himself **all** things, whether things on earth or things in heaven, by making peace through his blood, shed on the cross.* (Colossians 1:20)

All of humanity has been included in what Christ has done. The Holy Spirit has indeed fallen on *all* flesh. As people hear this claim of belonging and inclusion on their lives, their antenna is primed to pick up free God Wi-Fi— and their lives are finally beginning to make sense! *They are going with the grain of life, not against it. And life is beginning to finally "work" and bear fruit.* It's no longer us against them. It's us together with them in perfect reconciliation already *in* Christ.

Indeed, "God was reconciling the world to himself in Christ, not holding their trespasses against them, and he has committed to us the message of reconciliation" (2 Corinthians 5:19). He's calling us to go forth as "Christ's

---

* On the cross.

ambassadors" (2 Corinthians 5:20), forgiving one another as God in Christ has forgiven us (Ephesians 4:32).

How refreshing to get past the words of doctrinal and cultural differences and get back into discovering who is actually intuitively receiving and sharing the Spirit of ConneXion for all of us—it's our human brother, the Son of God! Christian churches may even drag their feet in relation to this truth, but it is time for new wineskins. We are being called to participate in the culture transcending movement in Christ that is already happening when we walk by faith and not by sight---when we walk in that which already is, and as it exists perfectly in the Person in the living Christ.

New Life for ConneXion

Originally, I thought the idea of ConneXion would evaporate into the mist after I was fired. In fact, the very week it happened, it came back to life. Here's how.

I found myself in a lawyer's office wrangling out some legal issues necessitated by action taken by our former denomination. I got an unexpected phone call. "Pastor Jim," a rather heartfelt charismatic Christian acquaintance said, "The Holy Spirit told me to call you. He told me to tell you you're supposed to call this lady about a building she owns that you're supposed to go see."

That week was so crazy. I figured anything that came up like this was a direction from God. Perhaps, I thought, this was the building to which God would lead us to eventually hold services with the group that wanted to form a new church and include us in it.

"Ok," I said. "I'll call her."

That very moment, I did. A friendly professional voice answered, and we set up a time for an appointment for the very next evening. Less than twenty-four hours later, I was driving up to what I was sure was going to be a small building capable of housing the forty members I knew were wanting to meet for worship together. As it turned out, it was perfectly capable of housing those 40 members—to the tune of 1,100 square feet per member! It was a 44,000 square foot fully equipped state-of-the-art office building surrounded by ten acres just outside the downtown area that I once saw as my mission field.

The owner gave me a tour as if I were a potential buyer, and I kind of acted the part. I remembered how Abraham responded when he was told he was going to have a baby in his old age; he believed God, and God reckoned it to him as righteousness. And then I remembered how the virgin Mary had the good sense to say (in effect) "May it be to your maidservant as you have spoken," when she was told she was going to have Jesus. This recently fired pastor who'd just refused a severance check with conditions was being offered the opportunity to look at the building as if he really was a potential buyer.

"What the heck, why not?" I thought. I went along for the tour. I tried to not look like I didn't have the 1.2 million dollars, which was the sale price of the building. I hope that's not some form of passive lying. Then an amazing thing transpired. The owner of the building turned out to be a modern-day Lydia (Acts 16).

By the time this visit was over, she and I kneeled and prayed together. I remember the day a few weeks later when I boldly launched into my understanding of the Spirit of ConneXion. It turns out that I was preaching to the choir. It was a perspective that she long believed to be true, even if she didn't use the same words. We began to pray and dream of what that might look like for this jewel of an office center.

I sought the input of trusted spiritual leaders. One was Chuck Proudfit of At Work on Purpose based in Cincinnati, Ohio.[28] Another was Jeff McSwain, Christian theologian, author, and founder of Reality Ministries in Durham, North Carolina.[29]

As a result of looking for ways to live out doing ministry via the Spirit of ConneXion, a new relationship has emerged between me and this wonderful sister in Christ. A new business center has now opened operating on the concept of "living out" and "giving out" the Spirit of ConneXion. The building is called The Tipp Center, and its slogan is "connecting business, community, and entrepreneurs."* This owner not only leases business space for non-profits and for-profits but also graciously shares the facility as a "connection center" of sorts for a variety of community initiatives. It's rapidly

---

* My friend Jeff McSwain, who helped me articulate some of the earliest visions of this ministry, says it's really the "T.I.P.P." Center – the Trinitarian Incarnational Proclamation and Practice Center. My prayer is that it will become a local, regional, national, and international model for other such locations.

becoming a regional civic and cultural center. Two churches meet in the facility, including the one planted after our being terminated by GCI in 2017.

I retired from formal pastoring in 2021, and I now serve as a chaplain for the emotional and spiritual needs of the people using the building in any way I can be of service. I like to think that I encourage the occupants to recognize that there is more connection between the people in this connection center than they may realize! As of this writing, it is now 70% occupied.

It's a bold experiment that is showing promise, and it is already bearing fruit. People seem to sense the Spirit when they walk into the building. Secular events almost feel like an old-time church potluck after a very good worship service. People who walk in with world-weary faces leave smiling with the joy and playfulness given by the Spirit. You can begin to see the visionary wheels turning in people's heads as they grasp the vision and seek to connect the good that can come into the community by a center such as this.

Does Doctrinal Truth Truly Transform?

As a Christian, I had journeyed from my Greek Orthodox cultic roots into a full-blown worldwide cult, and from there as an ex-cult recoveree into mainstream evangelical Christianity. Having stammered through the fog of Evangelicalism's cultic individualism, I am discovering what it means to be a Christian in Christ. *Or, I should say, I'm discovering what it means that I was in Christ before I was a Christian.*

Here's the central truth I've discovered. Doctrine in and of itself does not transform. Partaking in the Divine Nature of Christ—the divinized Trinitarian nature of the Son of God who is also the Son of Man—does. I have begun to rest in the reality that I have always been "very good" (Genesis 1:31) in God's eyes, just as he created me, and that he was so committed to his work of creation that he furthermore embraced me, his fallen beloved son, at my very worst, redeeming me from all wickedness (Titus 2:14). To the extent that we wake up and smell this coffee of grace and truth, we are motivated by the Spirit of truth "to do the good works God has prepared in advance for us to do" (Ephesians 2:10). That kind of work is the epitome of being at work on purpose, in God's purpose.

Being a cult or more specifically being cultic is not just a problem I and my ex-denomination had (and sometimes still have). The modern-day Christian landscape has its own share of cultic behaviors. So do some very ancient strains of the faith still functioning today. Some of them are turning off non-Christians not only about us but about the Christ we claim we worship. We may set out to crusade "in the name of Christ," while unwittingly giving Christ a bad name.

Until we can submit in Trinitarian ways to the truths God has given us to share with each other, we do not have the right or capability to address the divisions in the world around us. All Christians were meant to be catholic—universal in nature—but not just "Roman" catholic. All Christians were meant to be orthodox—possessing right doctrine—but not necessarily just "Greek" (or "Russian" or "Coptic") orthodox. All Christians were meant to be evangelical—but not just American Evangelicalism-style evangelicals.

If we can come to realize that "reality" is not just the fading away dimension of our experience, but that the real "us" lives "in" the Reality in God and in Christ, then a great deal of security can be brought to Christians who are judging their standing with God based on their "individual" response as an "individual" to the Ultimate Individual, God.

Instead of individuals worshipping "the great monad in the Sky" (C. Baxter Kruger), we are *all beloved* "persons" in the three-person unity of God. We are in Trinitarian Oneness with God and each other in the reality of Jesus Christ.

The dynamic substance of Reality is found in Jesus Christ (Colossians 2:17). Jesus Christ is *your* "righteousness, sanctification, and redemption" (1 Corinthians 1:30) just because he is. When you know that you are righteous in Christ, it's much easier to accept your "wrongs;" the God full of redeeming love is committed to conforming you to his   Reality.

Chapter 18

LOOKING BACK, AND FORWARD,

AT MY CULT LIFE TIMES FOUR

You may have noticed the title of this chapter mentions four cults. The fourth cult is one I am still growing out of. Let me explain.

My wife Becky recently encouraged me to listen to a series of lectures by Richard Rohr* entitled *Where Are You?* that she was introduced to in her spiritual direction program. Rohr is well known in Christian circles and is responsible for the work of the "Center of Action and Contemplation."

In one of the lectures Rohr remarks:

> *If we are going to let go of all the rules that have guided us in the past, then we better be developing a clear sense of how our own brokenness can twist our perspectives. Those who are moving into this stage in healthy ways are willing to ask this hard question: How might I be a bigger problem to myself, and those around me, than I've realized?*[30]

Oh, dear me! Like Karl Barth was reputed to have said (in one form or another) "I thought I'd drowned the old man. But he turned out to be a very good swimmer."

My denomination certainly didn't know what to do with me, so they disconnected from me, just as I had disconnected (in some ways, immaturely) from them. I can't just point blame at others. I must look at some blame stemming from myself. More particularly, how did my false self, my flesh, the

---

* For further information please reference www.cac.org. The lectures were given in the Spring of 2009 at a retreat with the Spiritual Direction Association of Colorado https://www.spiritualdirectioncolorado.org/

"old man," make me more a part of the problem than the solution at the time?

Let us all ask ourselves some tough questions. How honest can you be about the cultic demands *you* have placed on others? Does conformity to the way you see things *have to be* the only way *you will allow it* to be before you will enter into relationship with your spouse, your boss, your denomination, your government, your children, your parents, your neighbor, your friends, and even your nemesis?

Have you learned to acknowledge your own cult? Is your family still imprisoned in the cult of *your* judgment? Have you learned to acknowledge the legalism of *your* law, some inner set of rules and regulations (your Levitical law) that *you impose* on yourself and others to engage in relationship with them? Can you acknowledge the whole self you and others have in Christ, and therefore better grasp your own limitations?

Can just suggesting that these things may be a possibility be enough to help you start groaning under the evil Pharaoh *you are to you* (and possibly others) and cry out to God to be set free? Or can it at least encourage you to go through your Deuteronomy, your second receiving of the law of your life, against the humbler backdrop of the broken self your life journey (your "Numbers") has revealed to you?

Where are you on your journey? Where would you like to be?

I seek to continue emerging from my cultic tendencies, against my deep-seated penchant to classify people in us vs them ways. Even with arguably better theology, I am still mired in an ongoing cultic struggle. You see, I have discovered now that all human beings are in Christ, where in the Spirit we may live in correlation to reality, the reality we all have *in Him*, the reality about us that "is found in Christ" (Colossians 2:17). But as long as I am in this world, I will war against the flesh, the carnal cult-think that is as old as Cain and Abel. Before coming back to further address this fourth, ongoing cult in my life, I wish to share my heart about the first three cults of my experience. As I hope is clear, my intentions are not only to call out the "us vs them" dangers of each, but also to show the presence of Christ's faithfulness, goodness, and blessing all along the way.

To My First Cult(ure)—My Greek Orthodox Brothers and Sisters in Christ

The Greek Orthodox Church is amazing. The people I knew and loved there are wonderful, loyal, witty and clever, fiercely intelligent, and often very, very funny. Laughter came naturally. You love, and you love fiercely. You never let go. You worship God with a liturgy, with a service where the people are serving God and expect to get nothing out of it other than the honor of serving.

My Greek Orthodox brothers and sisters, I love you! You started me out on what has been a profoundly beautiful spiritual journey. And the One who has been with me all these years is still a very Greek Orthodox God, the God who managed to bypass the Enlightenment and still retain His place as Pantokrator of all.* Whatever He says or wants is truth. He simply *is* the Truth. Period. You will always be a part of me wherever I go, for eternity. Like a little garlic, a little Greek orthodoxy goes a long way. It flavors well most of the time.

My Big Fat Greek Southern Fried Church was a wonderful place to grow up. If not for what I feel was a distinct calling from God to sojourn spiritually in other directions, I would have never left it. I would have striven to save and preserve it and advance it out of love and devotion for Mama and Daddy if nothing else. I would have always been the first in line to serve at the altar on Sunday. I'd sign up with joy in the fall for every Greek Food Festival. I would still have to repent (grudgingly) for at least mildly feeling everyone who is not Greek is, well, a barbarian (to be honest, I still do, occasionally). I would probably believe, in ways that showed, what Michael Constantine's character aptly observed in *My Big Fat Greek Wedding*: "There are two kinds of people—Greeks and everyone else who wish they were Greek."[31]

I've often wondered why *My Big Fat Greek Wedding* was such a hit. It was humorous and on point while offering universal and identifiable truths. The closing scenes of the movie were so warm and wonderful. By the time it was over, people who yearn for deep connection really did want to be Greek like

---

* *Pantokrator* does not mean all-ruler or all-governor but rather all-holder, and although emperors might have deluded themselves into believing that they were ruling the entire world, it is Christ who rules. They certainly had no grasp of every little event that unfolded anywhere on earth, and that is precisely what the Greek word *pantokrator* means: having a grasp of everything. <u>Pantokrator | The amazing name Pantokrator: meaning and etymology (abarim-publications.com)</u>

you! You always connected with those you love and who love you, and I believe this deep connectedness goes beyond your cultural heritage. It points to the Trinitarian communion, the context for every human life.

I'm grateful my initial spiritual formation was bathed in your Trinitarian roots, unspoken as they were. In the years of sojourning with my heritage, I never heard the depths of the meaning of that truth expounded upon, but you live it and give it. You live the love of the Trinity. Your actions testify to the wonderfully organic connection to the Trinitarian Life of God that undergirds all of our lives and all of existence.

What you teach is sounding so much like what quantum physics is discovering, and how wonderful it would have been to have been shown that possible intersection of science and faith when I was looking for proof of God's existence. How much more amazing would your Christian effectiveness be if you could *preach* what you practice, making the truth of our inclusion in the Trinitarian life of God more plain and accessible to many people today?

As for me, ever an orthodox Greek, I can't say enough good things about you! However, *my* experience with you was more cultural than spiritual. As much as anything, the Greek part of your name seemed to be more important than the orthodox part or even the church part. I remember Greek weddings. I remember Greek cooking. I remember Greek icons. I remember Greek accents. I remember Greek food festivals. I don't remember anyone teaching me the Gospel of Jesus Christ, ever. I knew it enough to identify with the sufferings of Jesus when I suffered at the hands of other children as a youngster. But I didn't really know it in its fullness, in ways that would have filled in so many gaps in my understanding.

When I was a troubled teen, you had so many ways you could have answered questions that plagued me when I feared God did not exist. I obviously had picked up something of your reverence for Christ through sheer familial osmosis. But I never heard explanatory words about how our fear of God translated to assurance against *my* fears. It was simply assumed as something that needed no explanation. But I needed more than the implicit answers that are baked into the experience. I desperately needed someone to explicitly show me how God was really there for me, relevant to my life, at a time of need. As the Apostle says, "How will they know without a preacher" (Romans 10:14). But your church culture (at that time and maybe just to me) was too preoccupied with retaining your Greek immigrant culture and seeking to protect your successful integration into the predominant culture of the day.

Yes, I learned about how to participate in the liturgy, but I never heard the Gospel that would have made the liturgy make so much more sense. Would the church be more fruitful if, armed with its deep understanding of the Cosmic Christ and the fascinating nuances of orthodox doctrine (the Trinity, *theosis*, etc.), it held accessible evangelical Bible studies to bring people to Christ before (or even whether) they brought these people to the liturgy at church?

It pains me to say this, but I want to share this with my Greek brothers and sisters. All too often, the Gospel message I hear coming from the Greek quarters of God's church is less about the Gospel of Jesus Christ and more about the claim of having the "one true liturgy." Could we be so proud of our liturgy that we proclaim our possession of it more than we proclaim a simple Gospel that would make Americans, as well as Greeks, want to worship the King of the Kingdom in profound and ancient liturgical and Trinitarian ways?

What would happen if you could take off your vestments, open your Bibles, and share your ancient theology with American people who doctrinally might still be swinging through the trees of the theological garden rather than learning how included they are in the Trinitarian life of God? (Don't be offended, my fellow Americans! That's a take-off of yet another funny quote from Michael Constantine's character in *My Big Fat Greek Wedding*.)

You're so busy with all the liturgies! The Jews were so busy trying to "keep" the ancient Passover Festival that they hurried up and "squelched" (actually murdered) the real Passover, Jesus Christ (John 18:28), so that they could "keep" the Festival that was supposed to lead them to believe in Him! Things like that can happen to liturgical people very easily. We can miss the "spiritual Reality" forest for our "cultural preferences" trees.

So that's my life lesson I share with you, my beloved Greek family. I pray it helps you to consider what is of Christ in your midst, in distinction from what is simply of your culture. If you went to work figuring out and deconstructing the more cultic, us vs them, aspects of your faith expression, I've got a feeling the aroma of Christ would spread from you like hotcakes. Or better yet, like baklava, which is probably Turkish, but somehow you managed to brand it as your own. Oh, what you could be doing with your amazing doctrine if you were willing to become less cultic.

To My Second Cult—My Worldwide Church of God/Grace Communion International Brothers and Sisters in Christ

When I discovered the Worldwide Church of God, and what appeared to be its very sincere and simple adherence to whatever they understood to be the plain truths of the Bible, I finally got back a sense of grandeur about God. It didn't matter that the teachings weren't exactly right, as time would tell. My spirit and heart were full as I dug into the Scripture. The way I was taught enabled me to do more than just understand things "about" God. It enabled me to *feel* God again. I had episodic experiences with Him where I felt His real, palpable presence through the written word, preparing me to eventually discover Him more deeply as the Living Word. Wow, I can't say enough about how deeply grateful I am for that journey.

And what about your wonderful church members? What a sincere people I met in congregation after congregation, at festival after festival. I had been looking for my brothers, looking for a people to whom I could belong, and who would love one another as people who obeyed the Bible loved one another. And for a very long time, they were that people. To my dear brothers and sisters from WCG and from our GCI days, I love you!

Yes, we believed Hitler was the evil world ruler to come of Revelation (he was one of many). I would imagine Putin is now high on the lists in some of our WCG splinter groups. I recently heard a man on the radio from a conservative religious background state his sincere belief that nanotechnology has been inserted into the COVID-19 vaccine and is giving world dominion seekers digital control of our very bodies. On one hand, "Give me a break!" On the other hand, we believed some crazy stuff too, fed to us by our founder.

Besides disavowing our unsound and even quirky-at-times doctrine, there is something more that needs to be noted about my brothers and sisters in WCG: theirs is a beautiful legacy of a wonderful people whose spiritual history has been sold short in the process of their doctrinal changes. For so many of them, even in Armstrong's day, it *was* all about God, God's truth, and radical responsiveness to His will. Their monotheism may have overshadowed their trinitarianism, but they believed in Jesus. In our denominational revisionist narrative, I think you and your sincere faithfulness have been minimized, as if the good has been thrown out with the bad. You and your parents-- your loved ones who raised you in such an atmosphere of zeal—really were wonderful Christians. Yes, you were Christians in a cult, but there is much to be praised and remembered. You don't need to be ashamed of your past.

It was your love for Spirit-breathed Scripture that led you to discover the New Covenant Christ and to be willing to dismantle a multi-million-dollar empire to boldly proclaim him and dismantle what was cultic about us. Perhaps we could have taught the world about how to discern "truth" more truthfully, since we had to learn that the hard way. Under the leadership of Joseph Tkach and the influence of theologians like Kyriakos Stravinides (Greek Orthodox!) and Thomas Torrance, we were even led to Trinitarian theology, which I believe was an Early Church Father's gift to us. The popular "You're Included" segments filmed in the headquarters studio were an effort to share these ancient truths with our body and with the world. In this effort and others, we approached a move towards new wineskins that I believe God wanted us to embrace. We were stewarding what we had from our former days of proven multimedia savvy.

Looking back, I think that for all the good in the changes, we didn't quite get to where we were being called to be. I believe that coming out of the cult we actually had things God wanted us to share with the larger Christian body, not just our passion for Holy Scripture but our deep sense of family (again, an unwitting testimony to the Trinitarian context of human life), and more directly a non-Evangelical, Trinitarian emphasis on the gospel.

Maybe instead of focusing on being accepted by Evangelicalism, God was calling us like David from the back fields to a leadership role. Maybe, like good yeast, we could help them discover Christ the same way we did, helping them to recognize their own cultic tendencies in the process. Imagine what would happen if we had developed enough inroads into society that we could articulately and convincingly speak of the danger of falling for conspiracy theories and spurious religious idle talk as so many frightened believers are doing today.

In the old WCG days, we didn't have to worry about being embarrassingly evangelical (we left that to those non-Sabbath-keeping types). Back then we prayed, paid, and went to the feast, where "important' denominational leaders gave us the "next" thing to focus our lives on for the year until the next feast.

We returned home, trying to live as we did at the feast as well as our finances allowed, and we prayed and paid until we got to go to the next feast, where "important" denominational leaders gave us the "next" thing to focus our lives on for the year until the next feast. We were always waiting for the wonderful world of tomorrow instead of making the world a more wonderful place now, "on earth as it is in heaven."

To me, however, after the glow of the initial acceptance of our historic changes, things took a curious turn. It seemed our relatively newfound grasp of the gospel of unconditional grace somehow combined with the leftovers of the "God will resurrect them and save everybody in the Last Great Day" theology. They somehow coagulated into a condition a friend of mine calls a "spiritual couch potato" theology. The pendulum thankfully swung away from legalism, but often too close to the other extreme of antinomianism. In other words, with "the changes" many of us discovered the indicatives of grace---but left the imperatives behind. The misdirected zeal of legalism did not always translate into the holy zeal of the Apostle who in 1 Corinthians 15:10 claimed, "I worked harder than all of them, yet not I, but *the grace of God* that was in me." For too long our reformation has been more about *what we don't have to do* in the law than *what we now do get to do* in Christ.

Finally, we have already discussed the challenges inherent to GCI's continuation of the original hierarchical polity that came down from WCG. Wikipedia is not necessarily a reliable source, but what it says here about the organization is true to my experience:

> *"Grace Communion International has a hierarchical polity. Its ecclesiastical policies are determined by the Advisory Council of Elders. Members of the Advisory Council are appointed by the President. The President, who also holds the title of Pastor General, is chief executive and ecclesiastical officer of the denomination. A Doctrinal Advisory Team may report to the Advisory Council on the church's official doctrinal statements, epistemology, or apologetics. The President may pocket veto doctrinal positions he determines to be heretical. However, the President is also a member of the Doctrinal Advisory Team, and so he is aware of and involved in the activities of that committee. Historically, Presidents, as chairmen of the board of directors, have appointed their own successor. This and the President's power to appoint and remove members of the Advisory Council have remained areas of concern even among those who applaud the church's doctrinal changes."*[32]

Get back to the plain truth. Get back to the passion for the Scriptures as your parents had done, just do it without the bad doctrine and without family-ignoring misplaced zeal. Become the people of the plain truth and the main truth once again, and of Jesus Christ, who *is* Truth, the Jesus Christ who uniquely reveals the Triune Persons keeping truth with each other and with humanity. Teach discipleship in a way that demonstrates biblically how the imperatives are found *inside of* the dynamic indicative claim made on us by our inclusion in the ongoing obedient sonship of Jesus for the world. Shed the individualism of Evangelicalism so that you might share Christ with the world in ways I honestly think only you are equipped to do.

To My Third Cult: American Evangelical Brothers and Sisters in Christ

First, a disclaimer. I admit that I have less "street cred" when it comes to making a critique of American Evangelicalism. I did not grow up in an American church, nor did I belong to a traditional Protestant denomination for forty years, so I recognize that just about everything about my Evangelical experience is interpreted through the baggage of my cult experience—we all entered the Evangelical world while still within WCG. I also recognize that the fresh air that I felt entering Evangelicalism after "the changes" with WCG was largely based on a contrast with the suffocating legalism from which we were escaping. Evangelicalism, I now realize with clarity, is not a place I want to hang my hat. It's complicated. I realize that I now tend to contrast Evangelicalism with the fresh air of Greek Orthodoxy the same way I contrasted WCG with the fresh air of Evangelicalism. Forgetting my critique a few pages earlier, I tend to be a revisionist about the perceived glory days of my Greek Orthodox roots and the robust Trinitarian doctrine there, compared with what Mama might call the "pinto beans"* of my Evangelical experience. As I hope you'll see most clearly in the Conclusion, despite some full-circle connections to Greek Orthodoxy, that is not where I want to hang my hat either. So please take my description of these Evangelical pinto beans with a grain of salt (garlic salt even, if you want to be wary of my ever-present "Greek" lens).

Evangelical friends, although you don't often articulate the Trinity or speak much about the Trinitarian life of God, God has blessed you in many ways. The manner with which you love your families, your brothers and sisters in

---

* Hearkening back to the story from my youth, where my Greek mama said I was lucky to not have an American mother like the lady down the street, because she'd be feeding me pinto beans three times a day.

Christ in community, witnesses to the Trinitarian life of God in powerful, if not always conscious, fashion.

Unfortunately, against what I consider to be healthy elements of Trinitarian cohesiveness in your own communities, what I've seen in Evangelicalism is a strain of what I call "Declaration of Independence" Christianity. We feel duty-bound to defend and often declare our independence sometimes from God and very often each other. As Thomas Jefferson articulated, our American rebellion against the Mother Country was based on a contract, not a covenant. We were separate from England because that's what *we* had decided. We were breaking the contract because our Parent had broken theirs. The opposite side of this same coin is that just as we can break a contract when we decide, we enter a contract with someone only when *we* decide and not before.*

This contract mentality has infected Evangelical Christianity. The narrative begins with us separated (independent) from God, and sure, God has done his part of the contract, but we are not his children until *we* decide to secure our side of the contract. In effect, when *we* decide for Christ *we* are adopting ourselves into God's family, and only then do we have brothers and sisters in Christ who have done the same. There is no sense that we're already included in a covenant (not a contract) sealed from both the human and God side by the mediator Jesus Christ. There is no sense that we are already connected with every human being by virtue of Jesus Christ. All this makes us cultural aliens to the Trinitarian reality from which all life springs, the environment that relies on coinherence, not independence.

Before there was a universe, before gas and dust particles were created, or emanated out of God's being, before matter had mass and atoms had protons and neutrons circling a nucleus, there was baseline life. That life was Trinitarian—Father, Son, and Spirit—Three in One. It was not just that three eternal super-cooperative individuals had gotten together and agreed for everyone to always agree. Reality *was* Trinitarian. They were co-inherent—distinct and yet one.

---

* As Jeff McSwain reminds me, Evangelical Christianity is in this way Jeffersonian more than Lincolnian. Abraham Lincoln never acknowledged the secession of the Southern states. They *said* they were separating from the Union, but Lincoln said such separation was impossible. In his mind, the Confederate states always belonged to the Union, regardless of their insistence otherwise. This union was a covenant reality that could not change, no matter how fiercely it was opposed. Separation was an illusion.

Consider this explanation of "coinherence:"

> **What** is coinherence? The idea that two entities can be in each other and still be what they are. In-ness without merger. This concept comes from a theological source. The two natures of Christ, his divine nature and his human nature are each in the other, yet he is not a mixture of these natures, as each remains distinct.[33]

The Father, Son, and Spirit are a "communion." Communion isn't just something we simply *take*. It's what we *are* by virtue of the fact that the Being of our origination is a "communion," the three-in-one God that Christians call the Holy Trinity.

All life springs out of this communion. So, life is not just a bunch of created, stand-alone individuals agreeing (or perhaps merely compromising) on the rules in an attempt to function harmoniously while we all maintain our individuality. Life was designed to function in Trinitarian ways of being. God has included us as persons, not as individuals, in the Person of Jesus Christ in the Three Persons of the Trinity! The minimization of this Reality would be to perceive the individual as outside of this communion, as if one could decide to get out or get into it!

This driving individualistic force is the cultic expression of Evangelical Christianity.

We pay lip service to a God who is a Trinity, but we still function and live individually and not as the Trinitarian family of Being we were meant to be, including the intimacy we share with all of God's good creation, human and otherwise. We hide from God and each other with our boundaries of nation, gender, denomination, culture, and societal and individual fig leaves. We assume we can do whatever we want if we do it as individuals in the privacy of our own spheres and pretend it doesn't somehow affect the whole. We define our rights and hold onto them with fierce boundaries and tenacity. We deny the very Reality of the communion we are created for. Because the individual mantra means we determine and decide upon our individual inclusion (in this case salvation), we always live in some form of insular, cultic trap—some form of "us vs them." We miss the all-in-one and one-in-all kaleidoscope of glorious human coinherence and glorious human distinctiveness to note and share and celebrate.

The Life that Christ made known in his being as a "Son of man" or "Son of humanity" was simply *the Trinitarian life of God*. It's the life that our Enlightenment eyes of individualism simply do not allow us to see, until we see it! Then we marvel at the ultimate Reality we're all a part of, the reality of Jesus Christ that includes every human who has ever or will ever live or breathe.

Dear Evangelicals, we are so caught up in the idea of "us vs them" that we think *we* are bringing Christ to a person, community, or village---when instead *we can celebrate the fact that He's already there*! All we have to do is show them where he already exists in their lives and help them build upon that. We are all connected in the Son and Spirit of God, beloved children of the Father. We just have to let the Triune God show us how to speak each other's language in this fabric of shared life together. This makes us *more* evangelical, not less. We have such good news to share!

People from your churches are not radically winning over our culture. Evangelicalism has just become a sub-culture identity marker all its own. Increasingly, this causes you to speak in "us against them" terms about those who aren't part of you. There is little acknowledgment that Jesus is not only the light of the world (John 8:12), but the light that gives life to *every human* (John 1:9).

We spoke about Jesus feeding us, as he fed the 5,000. Fish and bread are quantifiable consumer-oriented things that some people have more of, and some less, if at all. The idea of feeding on Christ, not just being fed by him, is the language of coinherence and intimacy that defies the quantifiable. The idea that we are all one in the bread of life (1 Corinthians 10:17) is not only incomprehensible but offensive to Western minds that start with "I" before "we." Trinitarian life is the whole before the part, the community before the member, the "because we are, I am." The difference between communism and true community is that in the latter the person is not lost in the crowd, but finds their greatest distinctiveness *as part of* Christ's Body.

Former "Bible Answer Man" Hank Hannegraf cites a lack of sacramental coinherence as one of the reasons he left Protestant Christianity for the Greek Orthodox Church.[*] He writes:

---

[*] There is great irony in the fact that the famous Protestant Bible "answer man" and "cult watcher" Hank Hannegraf has come to affirm Greek Orthodoxy. Did he move from my third cult to my first? Not really. First, not every Greek Orthodox church is the same. Second, my first "cult" has attracted many Protestants because it is changing from the Greek Orthodox church of my youth. To the extent that it has absorbed critiques such as mine above it has become a more viable and vibrant option for those who want to experience Jesus and the gospel personally in the midst of a liturgical, Trinitarian, setting.

In a word, it comes down to "theosis" (union with God) — my growing realization through prolonged prayer and extensive reflection that this transformative process — and ultimate transformation — is the very purpose of human life. What's more, I've come to realize that we can experience the real presence of Christ in the Eucharist. That Holy Communion, rightly understood and administered, is vastly more than memorial. It is the primary means by which we may become by grace what God is by nature. Or as Peter puts it, become partakers of the divine nature (2 Peter 1:4). Increasingly, I'm yearning to know not only about Jesus Christ as the way and the truth but also Jesus Christ as the way and the life (John 14:6).[34]

In highlighting Hannegraf's journey, I am not promoting Greek Orthodoxy as the answer, only to show that Hannegraf is moving in the right direction. Only when we are completely free from some form of a doctrine of "us vs them" when it comes to the Biblical truths of salvation, reconciliation, redemption, forgiveness, adoption, even theosis, are we free in the Church from this earmark of cultic expression.

The Evangelical playbook says Jesus is "the Way" that "we" can give our lives to God, or that he provides the way whereby "we" can "choose" to be Christians. But these are individualistic mindsets. Christ as the way either opens the door for us as individuals to walk in, or we open the door of our individual castle so that he can come in. But as we have already noted, very little is said about the idea that because we exist in Christ by virtue of creation (Ephesians 2:10), and even pre-exist in the mind of God (Ephesians 1:4), Jesus Christ is not only the Way to God, he is *the* Truth and *the* Life of every human being. He is literally *your* way, *your* truth, and *your* life (as Jeff McSwain would say).

As an Evangelical pastor, I found that in this individualistic, consumer-driven mindset, people in a congregation wielded great power over me as a pastor. This was a strange mixture, a hybrid of sorts, with the hierarchical model we were still struggling to get past. I found the following insight apropos because it describes what ended up happening to us: "In the denominational hierarchy, officers are unsure what their role really is. Whereas the role of bishop used to be that of "the pastor's pastor," the author now often hears of bishops taking sides against the pastor, and with the anxious immaturity of local congregations."[35] The people were empowered to hold pastors hostage because they could "vote with their feet" by leaving at any time, taking their "tithes and offerings" with them.

Much to my chagrin, many of my new congregants at CrossRoads didn't want the rigorous approach to scripture study that we had in the biblically addicted "cult" that enabled us, eventually (ironically), to discover Jesus and the New Covenant with such a passion that we gave up a whole religious empire for the "new truth" of Jesus. I discovered that hardcore, in-depth, biblical truth was a very hard sell. And I hate to say it but *sell*—in a very consumeristic cultural climate where it was a given that many people voted with their feet— was the operative word. Here I quote Ryan Aycock.

"People are indeed searching for meaning, but he adds: Unfortunately, if that search for meaning only goes so far – if a person is a spiritual baby left only to suck on the theological pacifier forever – then the church has failed in its primary role to help people grow spiritually."[36]

Ideas behind the Trinity, coinherence, our human union with God and with one another in Christ and the Spirit, these things are hard for a rugged Western individualist to swallow. The K.I.S.S. (keep it simple, stupid) approach is far easier and requires far less time than struggling with a God whose truths you don't immediately understand. Like Jacob (Israel), we Christians are meant to be people who struggle with, or wrestle with, God and his truth, the "mystery of Christ" (Ephesians 3:4, Colossians 1:27, Romans 16:25, 1 Corinthians 2:7, Ephesians 1:9, Colossians 2:2, Colossians 4:3, 1 Timothy 3:16). We're meant to care about it so much we're willing to not let God go until he "blesses" us---blesses us with the real Truth, Way, and Life---Jesus (Genesis 32:26, John 14:6)! And we're supposed to want to know Him more and more for the rest of our lives (Philippians 3:10) ---even if that means "participation in his sufferings, becoming like him in his death."

"The widow who lives for pleasure is dead while she lives," Paul wrote in 1 Timothy 5:6. Tragically, so is the pastor who has to live to "please" his or her laity so they won't leave and take away the church's funding. At least, that's the way they end up feeling on many a Monday morning after a Sunday where they wish they really could have taught the truth longer, or with less soft peddling, than they did the day before.

The cult of nontrinitarian individualism and high-demand consumerism hinders people from slowing down and reflectively receiving and believing in the Trinitarian life of God in such ways that they palpably emit it from the

164

core of their being. The Declaration of Independence mentality is the major cultural flaw, the most dangerous cultic tendency, that I've noticed in American evangelical Churchianity.

All of us are human. We're all to a degree self-centered and ethnocentric. We all have our human proclivities, biases, and prejudices. We judge others who are not affiliated with us or with our cause, or who do not believe what we believe. All of us who are Christians are to some degree *Christians in cults*, if nothing else our "own" *personal-way-of-seeing-things* cults. But we're simultaneously all *Christians in Christ.* If we can learn to discern the difference between the two and emphasize the latter rather than the former, we'll step through the cultic trappings "that so easily entangle" us "and run with perseverance" the race marked out for us, looking to Jesus, the author and perfecter of faith (Hebrews 12:2).* We will finally see that we are Christians in Christ because, first and foremost, like all people, we are *humans in Christ.*

To My Ongoing Fourth Cult: Myself!

As mentioned above, my fourth cult is the one right in front of my own nose, or even closer. It's ingrained in me, partly from the fall and partly from the journey through my other cults. I have found it's impossible for me to move past the us vs them mindset in one fell swoop! I am a broken and fallen person whose brokenness and fallenness cannot help but affect my perspective. Theologically I might believe that no us vs them really exists, but to the extent my day-to-day thoughts and actions prove otherwise, I am still caught in the struggle. I believe, help my unbelief!

As a young boy I rightly transferred my reliance on the safety of my parents' world to the safety of my spiritual Father—eventually. But I can also see how, in tandem with that, I gave myself additionally to a new set of sub-parents— to the hierarchy and security-promoting dogmatism of a tightly wound cult.

In recovery, I can see how controlling tactics generated by my fear and anger have played out in attempts to make others conform to my personal "cult" as well. If there are times when I am a Christian preserving some cherished (and probably idealized) cultural environment for safety and belonging, my sincere

---

* In some translations of Hebrews 12:2, the pronoun "our" is inserted before faith—making it read the "author and perfecter of *our* faith" ---falsely giving it an individualistic tenor, rather than the focus on Christ as the originator of all faith.

desire is to be a Christian living in eternal safety *no matter what this world throws at me* (John 16:33, KJV) simply because I'm *in* Christ!

Stepping into the fullness of my freedom hasn't been immediate, but it seems more accessible. I sense that I am coming more and more into my "own" in Christ. Thoughtful brothers with whom I can truly share Trinitarian transparency have helped me grow into that freedom.

My experience in Levitical Christianity was so black and white, so rule-driven. I was very active in my "cult" cult. I thought the cardinal "line in the sand" observance was the Sabbath. I lived in an "us vs them" world. I was even more active in my ex-cult's reformation and adoption of mainstream cultural Christianity and sought security in achievement by the new rules, whatever they might be. But I could never quite master just what those Evangelical rules were. In the end, they proved to be rules that promoted a very consumeristic, market-driven approach.

It seems our "culturally" successful versions of Christianity are not designed to break people free from this level as much as leave them stuck in it. As a pastor I got trapped in an endless loop of people coming, going, coming again, and going again. It was a cycle in which I am still stuck to a degree, but thankfully I am learning to resist performance traps and am finding more authentic and fruit-bearing ways to serve Christ.

Because of my confusion in resisting the "cheap grace" of my Evangelical world, and because of not knowing how to best navigate virtue and ethics, I at times found myself yearning for the joy and security I felt more in the God-first, Bible-first cult of WCG. I was like the Israelites in the wilderness more than occasionally wanting to go back to the safety, security, and familiarity of "slavery" in Egypt (Acts 7:39).

I wonder if that's why the Israelites (and we) had to wander so long in their wilderness in what I call their "Numbers" phase.* Languishing in a culture of

---

* It seems we all begin with a "Genesis" of some sort, until some sort of relational issues force us into an Egypt for a while. Then, what at one time was good for us (Egypt) becomes a place of slavery. Then we need to experience an "Exodus" of some sort. After we do, it's easy to become very rule driven, go through our own "Leviticus" of rules and regulations we impose on ourselves and others. But a "perfect" number of years of wandering around in a wilderness learning and relearning the same life lessons repeatedly until we get it (our "Numbers" phase) leads us to a happy place of a more wisdom based "reception" of our life law (our Deuteronomy phase). Then finally, we may just be ready to let Jesus (our Joshua) take us into

bondage and ex-bondage, the Israelites had a lot of adolescent processing to get out of their system in the wilderness. Both my ex-cult and I had a lot to process in those "post-changes" years. It was impossible for any of us to avoid operating out of places of trauma and immaturity, and this manifested more in some instances than in others.

I was told that one of the most common pitfalls of folks who have been "kicked" out of ministry, as we were, is that they give up on God, themselves, and others and, I would add from personal experience for a while, be tempted to turn on all three! It took a long time to bring things into focus and for my crushed spirit to begin to revive. Thankfully, I've stopped projecting blame; well, at least sometimes I have.

But be forewarned that when God frees you from a cult, whether it's one you've belonged to or simply the cult of *you*, it's not going to be easy. You may give up on God for a while and other Christians, too. You may give up on yourself for a while and do the only thing left to do: accept your "death" and enter the tomb of waiting and rest with the Saturday Jesus.

If you're in this phase, try to endure and maybe even enjoy the wait. You're stuck there anyway. And if you can't do what you want, do what you can. Take up a new hobby. Dye your hair if you've always wanted to but were scared to try. Make a new friend.

I remember going rafting with some brothers, and when we'd hit a series of rapids, we'd all row like crazy to negotiate our way to calmer waters. One time, our guide said simply, "Next time, do nothing." We did and guess what? We simply enjoyed the ride, and the waters smoothed out.

God is in your boat, speaking peace while with you in the center of the storms of life. God has known who "you" *really* are all along, and still loves you. The reality is that *you are* alive in Christ and that there's more to come. The God who has us join him on the cross shares his resurrection as well.

It has been tempting to go back to older, more legalistic ways of functioning. I know that would be wrong. After a while, as you access Christ's life for you more and more, and let him explain yours to you in the context of him, your defeat—whether it's being fired, divorced, loss of your dream, coming face

---

the Promised Land and begin to receive our inheritance in the Kingdom of God---which has always been so near (Mark 1:14). At least, that's a pattern that has spoken to my journey.

167

to face with some kind of moral weakness that is really in you with humiliating honesty, whatever—your defeat, your cross, becomes your glory.

I recently stepped down from my role as pastor of the church that was formed right after I was fired as a pastor, and graciously, gave me a place to preach. It wasn't that I didn't love these people or them me. We just were at different places in our journey, and I could no longer authentically pastor them and be true to who I was, frankly, because I'm not quite sure I even know exactly who I am yet. But the True Self has emerged just enough to know that I could no longer be living out the persona of the now-dead false self. And I'm truly excited about fresh discoveries concerning who I really am and am meant to be, in Christ, and with whom I belong.

I feel humbled by my journey. I can see so many faults in me that I can't be too hard on others truly pointing them out. In fact, I could probably flesh them out with even more detail than they're able to articulate.

Delving deeply into the Trinitarian writings of Karl Barth, peppered heavily with quotes from Julian of Norwich, in an upcoming work by Jeff McSwain (see Appendix), has helped me move past the guilt and shame I feel about my confusion. It is growing into an ever-increasing source of joy.

Some days I'm there, and "the fig leaves" of shame are being discarded, or at least they are hanging more loosely, and I'm not tending to them as much as I once did. But be careful to whom you choose to reveal yourself at this phase. Joseph had to put his brothers through a few tests before he "made himself known" to them.

I thought my ex-cult community would fill that bill, but God has shown me other brothers to whom I do belong. And I'm now learning how to find them in all kinds of places. Hopefully, as God grows more Christians in Christ and not in cults, we will all be able to be that brother or sister to others in that way and find healing within our own families as well.

My deepest desire is to just be who I am in Christ. I want to be defined not by what others think about me, and not even by what I think about me, but by what Christ thinks about me. I'm not there all the time; I am *sometimes*, or at least I can taste it. And it is great. On a good day, when I'm living out of my center *in* Christ, I'm there. But there are bad days too. It's so much better to face the bad days *in* Christ rather than in an immature cultic environment that forces me to deal with my brokenness in self-rejecting hopeless ways.

Tomorrow is always another day. It's almost always fresh and beautiful. I know there is more to come. I look forward to continuing growth edges.

Conclusion

AN ONGOING GROWTH-
EDGE—*HUMANITY* IN CHRIST

For years I had a cultic view of Christianity. I believed that I was *in* Christ because I was in God's one true church, whether it be the Greek Orthodox Church, Armstrong's Worldwide Church of God, or the Evangelical Church (GCI). I now realize that those things are not the reason I was *in* Christ.

During the WCG phase of my journey, I believed I was *in* Christ because I found out the right "elemental" things he wanted me to do (things that pertained to the "elements" of this world, like the Sabbath, the Holy Days, etc.). Christ kept those things (as was appropriate to his mission and culture), and so should I---or so I thought. I was a Christian because I was doing things correctly the way he wanted me to do them, both from the Old Testament and the New—from the whole Bible. But I came to see that's not the reason I was *in* Christ.

In the next phase of my ministry, I entered the world of mainstream evangelical Protestant Christianity. What a Disney World of spiritual roller coaster rides that was! There were so many rides to choose from. The lines to get to those rides were long and crowded, and the days in them were hot and exhausting. Yes, I had entered something considered by many to be a doctrinally orthodox world, but that's not the reason I was *in* Christ.

What is the reason?

Simply because by generating me into being in himself, Christ has put me---and all humanity---there. And he does the same for you, too. In him we live and move and have our being!

170

The Bible tells me so.

For in him we live and move and have our being.' As some of your own poets have said, 'We are his offspring.' (Acts 17:28)

The Cretan poet Paul was quoting here, Epimenides, lived some 600 years before Christ was born. The timeless truth is that Epimenides himself lived and moved and had his being in Christ, and perhaps "intuitively" knew these words to be prophetic. Deep down inside, you and I do too.

In the Spirit, and in spite of our cultic-minded flesh, we now have the opportunity to believe and embody the gospel!

We Are All *in* Christ!

Now I recognize that I am a Christian like a flower stems from the root. In other words, my Christian faith is an expression of the fact that I am one human among all humans who have his existence and being *in* Christ. I believe you are in Christ too. He is the root of your life, whether you know it or not, and whether you are a Christian or not (as Jeff McSwain constantly reminds me, there will be no "Christians" in heaven, only people participating in Christ).

We are not "in Christ" because of our label as "Christians," or because of our culture, or our cultural practices, or our Enlightenment-driven "self" acceptance of him, and certainly not because of our red, white, and blue cultural affiliations.

We are not in Christ because we've formed a worship community or joined an existing one.

We are not in Christ because we have assented to a life of faith and community focused on him.

We are not in Christ because we have chosen the Christian religion for whatever propositional truth that sold us on it as the best faith option.

We are not in Christ because we have joined the Jesus Club by having come to believe "in" Christ.

If all humans are in Christ, does that make all humans Christians? No! Christians desire to play by the rules of Christ's reality, and in correlation to the belonging given us by grace in the one who calls us his beloved. I can go with Christ in the Spirit of Christ, or I can resist the Spirit, piercing myself with many griefs (1 Timothy 2:10). I cannot undo what Christ has done and who he has made me to be, but I can deny him to my destruction (2 Peter 2:1).

Our lives fluctuate in obedience and disobedience, but one thing stays the same: Jesus' unconditional love. The Bible tells me so.

Ontological Trinitarian-Based Reality

We all live and move and have our being *in* Christ (Acts 17:28).

We consist, subsist, hold together, and have mass *in* him (Colossians 1:17).

Our real lives are hidden *in* God, *in* Christ (Colossians 3:1-3).

When Christ, who is our life, appears, we will also appear in glory (Colossians 3:4), because the world will then see what we've always been—*in* Christ.

On that day, says Jesus, "You will *know [realize]* that I am in the Father, you are in me, and I in you" (John 14:20).

He didn't just make that union happen when we, as stand-alone individuals outside of him, came to believe in him. He made that happen before the foundation of the world—*in* Christ!

Before the foundation of the world, we have all been blessed with every spiritual blessing in him in the heavenly realm (Ephesians 1:3)—*in* Christ.

We were chosen before the foundation of the world to be holy and blameless in God's sight (Ephesians 1:4)—*in* Christ.

We have lived for who knows how long in the three Persons of the Trinity (John 14:2)—*in* Christ.

He is our Reality (Colossians 2:17) ---hence the reality of our being (our "ontology") is an "ontological Trinitarian-based reality"---*in* (you guessed it!) Christ.

What he's done, we've done, what he does as our high priest, we do, because we are in Christ! It's like kids in the car with Mom and Dad. Wherever they are going, you are going. That's how it is with Jesus. Where he's going, we are going. What he's doing, we're doing, even in our dim world in which we see through a glass darkly, and it's not always evident to us.*

Consider what we've been included *in*. When he died, we died. As 2 Corinthians 5:14 says, one died for all, so all died. Once again, all means *all*.

When he rose, we rose (Ephesians 2:6).

Christ did this apart from our verbal permission. When we were dead in transgressions, Christ died *for* us and *with* us in him (Ephesians 2:5).

The Bible says we respond to His Spirit in only two ways. Only two response words are used regarding the Holy Spirit. We can either *receive* or *resist*. We can either receive him, welcoming Reality, or resist him, resisting Reality. We can receive the forgiveness that has already been granted to us in Christ (Acts 26:18), or we can deny it, even though our denial doesn't make it untrue.

The Holy Spirit—Free God Wi-Fi—has indeed fallen on "all" flesh (Acts 1:17). That doesn't just mean some flesh, but all. It's like those downtown areas where there is free Wi-Fi everywhere. You might not be picking it up intentionally, you might not be logged in, and you might not have clicked "I agree" and typed in the password. But Jesus has said the "Amen" and "yes" to God for us all (2 Corinthians 1:18-22). This means that in reality you are always receiving Christ. That's the deepest reality. Our experience of this reality is up and down. On a good day, it feels like we're living more congruently with reality. Sometimes it just happens, intuitively. After all, that is the way we are naturally created to be *in* him. In the Spirit we receive him and represent him as ambassadors of Christ!

We can receive our place allotted to us, our inheritance, our "allotment,"** the same way the Israelites received their tribal allotments in the Promised Land (Judges 13-18). Or we can consign ourselves to a "hell" of loneliness and unnecessary rejection by our stubborn declaration of our independence and individualism, and not receive the place and forgiveness that are ours in Christ (Acts 26:18).

---

* Biblically, consider this example. Levi was considered to have tithed to Melchezedek simply because he was in the "loins" of Abraham when Abraham tithed to Melchezedek (Hebrews 7:10). In other words, what Abraham did Levi did because he was "in" Abraham. Since we're "in" Jesus it follows what he does, we do too!

** Some Greek translations of the word translated "inheritance" refer to it as 'the enjoyment of the allotment," which is what the word "kleronomos" somewhat woodenly means.

The lives God has given us to sojourn no longer have to be lives that are always only ready to happen, lives of promises stuck in a future Promised Land and inaccessible to us here in this world. Empowered by the Spirit, we can live lives of blessing now as the people God has created and redeemed us to be, giving to and receiving from others who are also children of the Promise (that's everyone by the way!). This promise to every human being is one that begins now because it's a promise that has always been. From our creation in Christ (Ephesians 2:10) forward, we can say the Kingdom of Heaven is near, in Christ, in whom we live.

Our new perspective reframes any "conquering" we do in Christ's name:

Glory, glory to the lamb!

You take me into the land.

We will conquer in your name!

And proclaim that Jesus reigns.

No longer is it a battle where we are conquering "enemy" nonspiritual "others" in the name of a spiritual "us" in Christ. It's more a matter of taking the sword of truth and slaying the lies of Satan who has deceived us all into seeing ourselves and others in this "enemy" light. We can proclaim the good news of Jesus Christ that really is good news: you belong, therefore believe!

We can discover who Jesus Christ is and therefore who we are. We can find our true identity *in* Christ.

If we can rise above the imposition of all our own cultic cultures on ourselves and others, we can begin to live—and give—God's gift through us to anyone with unbounded joy, no matter what happens next.

I don't want to be a Christian in my own or anybody's cult anymore. I want to live out of who I am---and all humanity is---in Christ. I want to live out of my---and *everyone's*--- true center more every day.

Where are you on your journey in Christ?

ABOUT KHARIS PUBLISHING

Kharis Publishing, an imprint of Kharis Media LLC, is a leading Christian and inspirational book publisher based in Aurora, Chicago metropolitan area, Illinois. Kharis' dual mission is to give voice to under-represented writers (including women and first-time authors) and equip orphans in developing countries with literacy tools. That is why, for each book sold, the publisher channels some of the proceeds into providing books and computers for orphanages in developing countries so that these kids may learn to read, dream, and grow. For a limited time, Kharis Publishing is accepting unsolicited queries for nonfiction (Christian, self-help, memoirs, business, health and wellness) from qualified leaders, professionals, pastors, and ministers. Learn more at: https://kharispublishing.com/

Appendix:

RESOURCES THAT WILL HELP

The theology that I have attempted to articulate in this book did not spring out of thin air. I would be remiss if I didn't include those whom I consider cutting-edge thinkers in our generation who have informed my understanding of Scripture and, more importantly, of what it means to be a Christian *in* Christ.

I will start with my first primary source for all doctrinal truth. That would be the very holy and ever-expanding, ever-revealing written Word of God. It still is so crucial to me in understanding the truths about God—but I don't worship the Bible. The One I worship, the Living Word (Jesus) now guides me with new eyes through the Written Word. And that is scary sometimes.

Reading the Written Word through the Lens of the Living Word

For most of my life, my main resource has simply been Scripture. I have read it in bite-sized chunks, obsessed over long portions in daily study, and visualized it through ever-improving lenses of clarity. It was originally through connecting with Scripture in WCG that I regained a sense of the reality of God's existence and His active engagement with my life. For years I read it as if all the commands of the Bible, on both sides of Jesus' birth, applied to me. Hence, I've kept everything from the Sabbath and Holy Days and three tithes and the food laws to the Lord's Supper and foot washing in a "to the letter" and elemental kind of way. That is, until I learned about reading them through the lens of Reality—Jesus, the one who is the "Word" become flesh, *the* Living Word.

The apostle Paul, in 2 Corinthians, explains this. Speaking about the way the books of Moses were understood by the Jews living after the resurrection of Christ, he said this:

14 But their minds were made dull, for to this day the same veil remains when the old covenant is read. It has not been removed, because only in Christ is it taken away. 15 Even to this day when Moses is read, a veil covers their hearts. (2 Corinthians 3:14-15)

You can read the Bible, but until you "see" Jesus and read it through the lens of the Eternal Word of God, you're going to get the written Word wrong. It will be in a well-meaning, Tree of Knowledge way, but it will still be wrong until you learn how to read it through the lens of Jesus. Paul continued:

16 But whenever anyone turns to the Lord, the veil is taken away. 17 Now the Lord is the Spirit, and where the Spirit of the Lord is, there is freedom. 18 And we all, who with unveiled faces contemplate the Lord's glory, are being transformed into his image with ever-increasing glory, which comes from the Lord, who is the Spirit. (2 Corinthians 3:16-18)

The author of Hebrews confirmed this in the first chapter of that book:

In the past God spoke to our ancestors through the prophets at many times and in various ways, 2 but in these last days he has spoken to us by his Son, whom he appointed heir of all things, and through whom also he made the universe. 3 The Son is the radiance of God's glory and the exact representation of his being. . . (Hebrews 1:1-3)

The written Word is amazing, yet it's misread and seen "through a glass darkly" unless it's read through the lens of the revelation of the glory of God in the face of Jesus Christ, the Living Word.

6 For God, who said, "Let light shine out of darkness," made his light shine in our hearts to give us the light of the knowledge of God's glory displayed in the face of Christ. (2 Corinthians 4:6)

So very simply, read the Written Word through the lens of the Living Word. Interpret Scripture considering who God really is and based on God's revelation of who we really are in Christ. Read them as someone who is living by Jesus, the Tree of Life. Jesus Christ is God's latest and greatest revelation of himself. The Son tells us more about the Father than any of the words in either the Old Testament or New Testament:

"No one has ever seen God, but Jesus Christ, his one and only Son, has made him known." (John 1:18)

As the New International Version puts it so beautifully, all religious practices up to the incarnation were just shadows of what was to come. There is a deeper way to truth!

*". . . **reality** is found in Christ."* [emphasis mine] (Colossians 2:17)

Reality *is* Found *in* Christ - The Works of Jeff McSwain

One of the greatest resources I've found in all my years for understanding the meaning of that Reality are the works of Jeff McSwain. I first met Jeff in 2010 and sought him out specifically after he had completed six segments of GCI's "You're Included" video series. Our denomination had begun studying Trinitarian incarnational theology as espoused by the works of theologians like Karl Barth and Thomas Torrance, among others. It emphasizes how we've been included in the Trinitarian life of God from before the beginning of time.

While the documents produced by the denomination were well done and made for intriguing talking points, something was missing. I could not resonate with their way of fleshing out the ramifications of Trinitarian theology in our lives now. Still (perhaps forever) healing from legalism in real or presumed ways, again their emphasis seemed to me yet another reason to stress what we don't have to do anymore because we are in Christ.

It seemed to me to be used to further legitimize preferred lifestyle choices very similar to the non-evangelical days of our cult years. We prayed. We paid our tithes. But we didn't engage in evangelism in our "now." God would take care of that in some later period.

Jeff, on the other hand, explained Trinitarian incarnational theology in a way that resonated with what I saw biblically happened after a formerly legalistic Paul discovered Christ and what I saw personally happen after I experienced Christ. It made you want to do more for him---not less! Jeff's explanations include a far more robust version of active participation in the Trinitarian life of God. So does his life example.

Jeff is the Founder of Reality Ministries, Inc., in Durham, NC (founded in 2007). The nonprofit's mission is "creating opportunities for teens and adults with and without developmental disabilities to experience belonging, kinship and the life-changing Reality of Christ's love."[37] At the Reality Center, adults of all abilities share life together in a myriad of ways.

I visited this center in 2017. In a faith-inspired atmosphere, the fruits of the Spirit are made evident in both those with and without disabilities in tangible ways. The palpable presence of the Trinitarian life of God is the reason why. The first tenet of the theological grounding of this highly fruitful ministry is what McSwain calls "a Christ-Centered View of Reality." "The Creator and God/human Jesus Christ," he explains on his website, "is the central truth of the cosmos" (Colossians 1:16-17). These central truths, among others, are listed in a section called "Theological Grounding" on the Reality Ministries website.[38]

He has published various articles and two books explaining this in detail. In *Movements of Grace: The Dynamic Christo-Realism of Barth, Bonhoeffer and the Torrances* (2010), Jeff says:

> To Barth, Bonhoeffer, and the Torrances, grace is not an abstract truth; it is reality itself. By God's revelation in Jesus Christ we are given the blessed assurance to know that all human beings are included in the humanity of the Savior. And in Christ we discover the movements of grace, a double movement at once God-human ward and human-Godward, all by the Holy Spirit. These theologians were keen to remind us that Christ's ongoing mediatorship includes all appropriate human responses to God. In fact, only by grace and in union with Christ do we have true response-ability. It is this "going with the flow" of the Holy Spirit en Christo that makes Christo-realism so dynamic and life-giving.[39]

Jeff's second book is *'Simul' Sanctification: Barth's Hidden Vision for Human Transformation* (2018). This work is described in this way:

> Why do we see so much fruitful good in unbelievers and so much evil in believers? What could it mean for a believer that the old is "gone," especially when it doesn't feel that way? What does it mean for humans who are simul iustus et peccator (simultaneously righteous and sinner) to be transformed in Christ and by his Spirit? We typically think of sanctification as pertaining to humans being conformed to Jesus, but what could it mean when Jesus speaks of himself as being sanctified for our sakes (John 17:19)? Jeff McSwain mines the theology of Karl Barth to engage such questions. In looking "through the simul," he concludes with Barth that universal human transformation is a reality before it is a possibility, and that, despite our contradictory state, we may live Spirit-filled lives as we participate in Christ's true humanity that determines ours—a humanity which never gets old.[40]

Jeff's next project, a two-volume set, is aimed at "pastors and armchair theologians." I recently spent a year studying the drafts of *Hidden in Contradiction: Humanity in Christ Before, During, and After the Fall* and *The Goodness of Judgment: The Ministry of Christ's Cross for a Hurting World.* I am in the process of distilling each section, and I'm hoping to create a study guide including suggestions for further scriptural study.

All that said, this material has greatly influenced my thinking about what it means to be a Christian *in* Christ. Again, consider the first tenet discussed above as the "Theological Grounding" for "Reality Ministries":

> *"The Creator and God/human Jesus Christ is the central truth of the cosmos"*
> *(Colossians 1:16-17)."*[41]

I sincerely believe that he is.

This theology, as Jeff teaches and lives it, is transformative not only doctrinally, but experientially as well. Rather than being a theology that justifies a spiritual couch potato approach to life, the version McSwain espouses inspires a life of active service that one would think follows such participation in Christ's life. It has certainly borne fruit in Reality Ministries (realityminstriesinc.org), and in the North Street Neighborhood, an intentional community (17 houses) near downtown Durham where people of various abilities live life as neighbors (northstreetneighborhood.weebly.com).

I cannot recommend Jeff's books highly enough as a resource for discovering what it means to be a Christian in Christ. Many of the concepts I've shared have been influenced by his eye-opening teachings. You can learn more from his website: https://www.jeffmcswain.org.

"At Work on Purpose" – The Marketplace Movement founded by Chuck Proudfit

As I wrote earlier, God opened the doors of what is now called The Tipp Center almost immediately after my separation from our former denomination. It's a 44,000-square-foot fully equipped office building, and the owner, Sheila Ingram, immediately resonated with the ministry of connection in a marketplace setting.

When I realized this door had been opened for ministry with such an amazing location, it occurred to me that this opportunity needed to be shared with other Christians of like mind who wanted to bring the church to the community, and not just require the community to work its way through the inhibiting cultural layers of the church as we know it today.

I reached out to Chuck Proudfit because of a phrase he used to describe a thriving ministry he started called "At Work on Purpose." Without knowing all the things included in what is now an international ministry doing cutting-edge things in the marketplace in the name of Christ, to be "at work on purpose" sounded exactly like what Christians simply *in* Christ would be doing.

They would be "at work," for the Lord, and, whatever they did, they would do "on purpose" for him. They'd be doing their jobs not just as sources of income but as ministries done by, through, and for Christ. The workplaces they would go to would become places where people would meet each other, and, in the bond of the Spirit, where inspired collaboration might take hold. What if, instead of being preoccupied with "return on investment," these people find themselves operating in a Kingdom economy? In the anointing of the Spirit, the so-called secular water of their efforts is turned into the wine of Christ. God's Word, Christ Jesus himself, will not return void.

It's striking to consider just what it means in the market and workplace when we begin with every person in Christ and indwelt by the Spirit. The Spirit provides exciting anticipation for what God might do in and between people and how, across church and business sector lines, people can corporately and collaboratively influence their communities.

Chuck describes his ministry this way:

> *At Work on Purpose has emerged as an innovative citywide workplace ministry model that mobilizes the Church at Work across church homes, denominations, zip codes and ministries. While we remain headquartered in Cincinnati, we are now supporting the development of citywide workplace ministry across the world.*[42]

This is a culture-transcending ministry being promulgated by Christians at work and living life on purpose in Christ. You can read more about it in the link shared in the note for the quote I just cited.

"Healing and Whole-ing" – The Healing Care Approach Founded by Terry Wardle

My wife Becky has been on quite a journey of spiritual discovery and recovery herself. She, too, made her way to faith facing great opposition from a "faith-less" family of origin to become a passionate follower of God committed to helping others learn how to grow awareness of God's love and faithfulness in their lives and follow Him more faithfully as well.

She was asked to leave her home by her parents when she chose to begin attending church with the Worldwide Church of God in what for her was a true response of sincere obedience to God. The fruits of God's Spirit have been in her in many ways.

I still can't believe she married me, even though she never wanted to marry a pastor. She served zealously in our church, especially through the rebuilding years after our doctrinal transformation. She took a full-time job, in part to enable our family to have insurance since the church we were pastoring, growing though it was, could still not afford to insure us. She not only worked tirelessly by my side but behind the scenes as well. She, too, went through a period of great mourning, a sense of betrayal, and loss from what happened to us after our forty years of service to the Lord with our denomination. She also found a great sense of healing in the Lord because she was growing in being a Christian in Christ, and not a cult.

Once she'd gotten back on her feet, she searched for new ways to serve Him and to access spiritual healing. She found a source that helped her forgive those who had hurt her. One unforgettable epiphany was in a "healing prayer" experience. She saw, in her mind's eye, exactly where Christ was in the pain and hurt---not just for her, but for those who'd hurt her as well.

From that point on, she found the peace and strength to move on and forgive. God knew what was done. God cared. And God took vengeance on it—in Christ. She found a vehicle for helping others who need to do the same. She was able to do this, in part with the help of Terry Wardle's Healing Care ministries, with whom she was going through training to become a spiritual director.

The fruit of this ministry is real and reflects what Christianity is like when it's not done through the lens of a culture but of Christ himself, and it helps people see where Christ was with them in their past in ways they may have not recognized before.

I'll let Terry tell the story of how this very "in Christ" ministry came about.[43]

My story begins at a crossroads. Not at a stop sign or traffic light, but at the intersection of brokenness and blessing, the place where wounds meet healing, and light blinds darkness in the presence, power, love, and truth of Jesus Christ.

By the early 1990's I had planted one of the fastest-growing churches in the United States, been the head of a theological seminary, written books, and had an international speaking itinerary. I was headed for the top rung of the Christian leadership ladder. But as the external pressure collided with internal turmoil (another crossroads) I spiraled into a debilitating breakdown that landed me in a psychiatric facility in Colorado Springs, Colorado. Instead of climbing the ladder of success I began to descend into a journey not of my choosing. A journey where I wrestled with unaddressed issues from the past. A journey of increasing intimacy with God. A journey that demanded that I lean into a trusted community.

As time passed, my transformation became apparent to family, friends, and church community. I began to speak publicly about God meeting me in the darkest places in my life and healing deep emotional wounds. That deeply personal experience became the framework for a new approach to helping hurting people find healing and wholeness in God. I began to interweave what I learned from the behavioral sciences with practices of Christian spirituality; eventually creating what now is called Formational Prayer.

These insights moved from one-on-one sessions to small group discussions, from weekend retreats to our first official training event. Those humble beginnings became a movement that seeks to empower Christians on the journey to wholeness.

For the last two decades, my organization, Healing Care, has hosted events throughout North America, equipping thousands of professional counselors, pastors, physicians, and lay leaders to help hurting people experience healing in Christ.

Of particular note is this ministry's insistence that Christ is near to the broken-hearted. Christ is for us. The Christ of the Cross is our contemporary. Christ is outside of time and space and can enter our hurts, past, present, and future. Such prayer "in him" can help lead us not only to healing but to the wholeness we were all created with *in* him.

We are whole! It's because we are *in* Christ. We can participate both in the "healing" and "whole-ing" that come from him, both now, and for eternity. We are always his beloved because all of us have been beloved since our real beginning---in Him!

WORKS CITED

Preface: Cultic Christianity

[1] Byrnes, Hristina. "17 of the Most Terrifying Cults in History." *MSN*, MSN, http://www.msn.com/en-us/news/world/17-of-the-most-terrifying-cults-in-history/ss-AAQ4gNO. Accessed 28 October 2021.

[2] "Cult." *Merriam-Webster*, Merriam-Webster, https://www.merriam-webster.com/dictionary/cult. Accessed 23 July 2022.

Chapter 4

[3] Manis, Andrew. Religion, Belonging, and Social Mobility in Civil Rights Era Birmingham, Alabama. Department of American Studies, Aristotle University.

[4] Martin, Walter R. *The Kingdom of the Cults*. Bloomington, Bethany Fellowship, 1965.

Chapter 5

[5] Tucker, Ruth. *Another Gospel: Alternative Religions and the New Age Movement*. Grand Rapids, Zondervan, 1989, p. 193.

[6] *Ibid*. 193.

[7] *Ibid*. 194

[8] *Ibid*. 195

[9] *Ibid*. 205.

[10] Ibid. 206.

[11] Ibid.

[12] Ibid.

[13] Ibid.

[14] Herbert W. Armstrong, *The Autobiography of Herbert W. Armstrong,* vol 1. (Pasadena, CA: Worldwide Church of God, 1986) 340.

[15] Tkach, *Transformed by the Truth*, Multnomah Books, 1997, pp. 90-104.

[16] Armstrong, Herbert. *Pagan Holidays or God's Holy Days: Which?* Pasadena, Ambassador College Press, 1974., p. 4.

[17] Hagee, John. *His Glory Revealed: a Devotional*. Thomas Nelson, 1999. *Google Books*, https://books.google.com/books/about/His_Glory_Revealed.html?id=6Kym3Lyrf4IC. Accessed 22 July 2022.

Chapter 7

[18] *Zorba the Greek*. Directed by Michael Cacoyannis, performances by Anthony Quinn and Alan Bates, Twentieth Century Fox, 1964.

184

Chapter 8

[19] Streisand, Barbra. "People." *People*, Columbia, 1964, Track No. 12. Vinyl.

Chapter 9

[20] Waltari, Mika. *The Egyptian*. WISO, 1945.

[21] *"Transformed by Christ."* www.wcg.org. Accessed 3 Mar. 2001.

[22] Tkach, *Transformed*, 25, passim.

Chapter 10

[23] Fitts, Bob. "Victory Chant." *The Lord Reigns,* Hosanna Music, 1989, Track No. 3, CD.

Chapter 11

[24] https://www.christianitytoday.com/ct/1996/july15/6t826a.html.

Chapter 12

[25] Martin, Chris. "Stories of Transformation: Crossroads Christian Fellowship Improves Communication." *Christianity Today*, 2014, www.christianitytoday.com/edstetzer/2014/november/stories-of-transformation-crossroads-christian-fellowship-i.html. Accessed 22 July 2022.

Chapter 13

[26] Valekis, Jim. "Open the Eyes of Our Hearts, Lord, We Want to See Jesus." U of Montevallo, Master's Thesis, 2001

Chapter 14

[27] "How Do You Know You've Made a Disciple?" *SonLife,* www.sonlife.com. Accessed 13 July 2022.

Chapter 17

[28] *AtWORKonPurpose.* https://atworkonpurpose.org. Accessed 14 July 2022.

[29] *RealityMinistries.* https://realityministriesinc.org.

Chapter 18

[30] Eades, Wes. "Richard Rohr's Level of Spiritual Development–Part 3." *Practical Spirituality*, vol. 3, 2014. *Practical Spirituality*, https://practicalspirituality.wordpress.com/2014/02/16/richard-rohrs-levels-of-spiritual-development-part-3/. Accessed 22 July 2022.

[31] My Big Fat Greek Wedding. Directed by Joel Zwick, performances by Nia Zardalos, John Corbett, Lanie Kazan and Michael Constantine, Gold Circle Film, 2002.

[32] Brady, Frank, et al. "Grace Communion International." *Wikipedia*, https://en.wikipedia.org/wiki/Grace_Communion_International. Accessed 23 July 2022.

[33] Theology and Science: A Coinherent History of Ideas, part 1 - Interface (regentinterface.com)

[34] Hanegraaff, Hank. "Bible Answer Man Hank Hanegraaff about his conversion to Orthodoxy." *YouTube*, 3 Oct. 2018, https://www.youtube.com/watch?v=qOsDK_BleF8.

[35] Gilbert, Roberta M. *The Eight Concepts of Bowen Theory*. Leading Systems Press, 2006, p. 99.

[36] Aycock, Ryan D., *Megachurches: How the Individual's Search for Meaning Led to the Disneyfication of the Church*. 2003, U of Florida, Bachelor of Arts in Religion (*magna cum laude*), pp. 19-20.

Appendix

[37] *Reality ministries*. https://realityministriesinc.org/ about. Accessed October 2022.

[38] McSwain, Jeff. "Theological Grounding." *Reality Ministries*, Reality Ministries, https://realityministriesinc.org/theological-grounding. Accessed 10 September 2021.

[39] Magruder, Kerry. "Movements of Grace." Jeff McSwain, https://www.jeffmcswain.org/movements-of-grace-1. Accessed 10 September 2021.

[40] Simul Sanctification. https://www.jeffmcswain.org/simul-sanctification. Accessed 19 July 2022.

[41] McSwain, Theological Grounding, passim.

[42] *AtWORKonPurpose*. https://atworkonpurpose.org. Accessed 14 July 2022.

[43] Wardle, Terry. "My Story." *Terry Wardle*, https://www.terrywardle.com.Accessed 19 July 2022.

Printed in the USA
CPSIA information can be obtained
at www.ICGtesting.com
CBHW070026090424
6561CB00006B/13